Holly Chantler is an experienced older and vulnerable client solicitor with particular expertise in dealing with complex issues relating to mental capacity, financial abuse, powers of attorney, advance decisions and the Court of Protection (contentious and non-contentious matters). Holly holds a number of professional appointments and qualifications, including as a Court of Protection panel deputy, panel guardian and a director of national organisations Solicitors for the Elderly and the Professional Deputies Forum. She also sits on the Court of Protection Rules Committee and acts as a professional stakeholder for the Ministry of Justice, Office of the Public Guardian and Court of Protection.

A Practical Guide to Assessing Mental Capacity

A Practical Guide to Assessing Mental Capacity

Holly Chantler
Solicitor and notary public

Law Brief Publishing

Published 2021 by Law Brief Publishing, an imprint of Law Brief Publishing Ltd
30 The Parks
Minehead
Somerset
TA24 8BT

www.lawbriefpublishing.com

Paperback: 978-1-913715-75-5

PREFACE

This book is aimed for the benefit of legal practitioners who are inexperienced in dealing with mental capacity issues and providing a refresher for those with more experience. The first part of the book deals with legal theory, the second part offers practical guidance in assessing capacity and the annexes provide further resources and precedents.

Legal practitioners must be satisfied that their client has the requisite mental capacity to provide instructions and as such, it is an area of law that all practitioners must have some awareness of. For those who do not regularly deal with clients where capacity may be an issue, it can be a daunting prospect to know what steps to take. This book aims to provide practical solutions and confidence to practitioners in those situations.

The law stated in this book is correct as at 31 May 2021.

Holly Chantler
May 2021

CONTENTS

PART ONE	**LEGAL THEORY**	**1**
Chapter One	What Is Mental Capacity?	3
Chapter Two	Professional Obligations of Legal Practitioners	5
Chapter Three	Who Should Assess Capacity?	9
Chapter Four	When a Capacity Assessment May Be Required	11
Chapter Five	Mental Capacity Act 2005: The Principles	13
Chapter Six	Supported Decision Making	23
Chapter Seven	Mental Capacity Act 2005: Test of Capacity	27
Chapter Eight	Specific Tests of Capacity	31
Chapter Nine	Assessment of Capacity	45
Chapter Ten	Retrospective Assessments	51
Chapter Eleven	Challenging Capacity Assessments	53
Chapter Twelve	Vulnerability Factors	55
Chapter Thirteen	Case Studies	57

PART TWO	**PRACTICAL GUIDANCE**	**65**
Chapter Fourteen	Lack of Capacity	67
Chapter Fifteen	Who Is the Client?	71
Chapter Sixteen	Lack of Capacity – Next Steps	73
Chapter Seventeen	Costs and Fees in the Court of Protection	111
APPENDICES		**121**
Appendix 1	Resources	123
Appendix 2	Precedent Attendance Note (Assessment of Capacity Element Only)	125
Appendix 3	Letter of Instruction to an Independent Assessor	127
Appendix 4	Court of Protection Application Flowchart	133
Appendix 5	Deed of Appointment of New Trustee Pursuant to Section 36(1) Trustee Act 1925	135
Appendix 6	Precedent Section 54 Trustee Act 1925 Order	139
Appendix 7	Precedent Section 36(9) Trustee Act 1925 Order	141
Appendix 8	Precedent Deputyship Order	143
Appendix 9	Orders sought from the Court of Protection (Box 4.1 COP1)	147

PART ONE

LEGAL THEORY

CHAPTER ONE

WHAT IS MENTAL CAPACITY?

Mental capacity is the ability to be able to make a particular decision or action at the time the decision or action needs to be taken. This may include day-to-day decision making, as well as more significant decisions which may have legal consequences. Examples of more significant decisions, and those which will often involve a legal practitioner, include:

- buying or selling property
- making a gift
- making a will
- making a power of attorney
- entering into a contract
- conducting litigation
- dealing with a divorce and financial separation

Individuals may lack capacity to make some decisions but not others, on some occasions but not others. It can be particularly challenging where a client has fluctuating capacity; often as a result of a brain injury or mental health condition.

There are many reasons why a person may lack capacity to take a particular decision at a particular time, perhaps as a result of a cognitive impairment, mental health condition or drug use. Depending on the circumstances, a lack of capacity may or may not be an issue. Clients can also regain capacity and as a practitioner, you will need to be aware of this possibility.

CHAPTER TWO

PROFESSIONAL OBLIGATIONS OF LEGAL PRACTITIONERS

Legal practitioners must be satisfied that their client has capacity to give proper instructions. This obligation is supported by case law (see, for example, *RP v Nottingham City Council and Official Solicitor* [2008] EWCA Civ 4) and the SRA's Code of Conduct for Solicitors, including Rule 3.1 which states "you only act for clients on instructions from the client, or from someone properly authorised to provide instructions on their behalf. If you have reason to suspect that the instructions do not represent your client's wishes, you do not act unless you have satisfied yourself that they do". Rule 8.1 requires you to identify who you are acting for in relation to any matter (this is relevant when considering whether you can take instructions from a third party). Failure to follow professional obligations may have negative consequences for the practitioner and their firm.

This can be difficult where clients are not able to provide clear instructions, for whatever reason, and it is the role of the practitioner to ascertain whether the client is capable of giving instructions having taken all practicable steps to assist them to do so. Mental capacity may fluctuate and the client may lack mental capacity to provide instructions on some occasions but not others.

Doubts may arise as to the client's capacity for many reasons, including:

- the client's circumstances
- information the practitioner has been told in advance
- who arranges the meeting
- what the client says

If a formal capacity assessment is required (from a medical practitioner), the legal practitioner should explain to the client:

- the concerns they have regarding their client's mental capacity
- the purpose of the capacity assessment
- any implications if the client is found to not have capacity

The practitioner should obtain the client's written consent or express agreement to carry out the assessment and to instruct the capacity assessor. The client should also be advised of any cost.

The practitioner should take all reasonable steps to seek the client's consent for the capacity assessment to be carried out. If the client does not provide consent, the practitioner must explain to the client in writing that they are unable to act for them or alternatively the practitioner may, if it is felt appropriate, continue to act without a report. If the practitioner decides to do this, they must document their decision making clearly. The practitioner must also explain the potential consequences to the client, such as a subsequent challenge and the transaction being set aside by a court.

If the practitioner considers that a potential client lacks capacity to give instructions, they may be entitled to decline to act. If the practitioner does wish to act, they should identify someone who has authority to provide instructions on behalf of the client (such as an attorney or deputy).

For an existing client, a retainer will usually automatically terminate upon loss of capacity unless there is express provision otherwise.

Further guidance as to a practitioner's obligations can be found in the Law Society's practice note entitled meeting the needs of vulnerable clients (https://www.lawsociety.org.uk/support-services/advice/practice-notes/meeting-the-needs-of-vulnerable-clients-july-2015/).

Professional obligations: summary

- You must be satisfied your client is able to provide instructions
- If in doubt, obtain a capacity assessment specific to the decision in question (with your client's consent)
- If your client lacks capacity to provide instructions, you may be able to accept instructions from someone authorised to act on thcir bchalf

CHAPTER THREE

WHO SHOULD ASSESS CAPACITY?

The person who assesses capacity will usually be the person concerned with the individual at the time the decision needs to be made. This may include the person's spouse, partner, carer, health professional or legal representative. If the decision to be made is serious or the outcome significant, a more formal approach may be required. Where there is doubt or a debate about capacity, it is ultimately a judicial decision (*Richmond v Richmond* [1914] 111 LT 273). Note though, the decision of Senior Judge Lush in *Re Collis* [2010] COP 27/10/10 (unreported) where he preferred the evidence of the solicitor (who acted as certificate provider in the making of a lasting power of attorney) and their assessment of capacity as it was the only evidence that was both issue-specific and time-specific, insofar as it addressed Mr Collis' specific ability to create a lasting power of attorney at a specific time. He went on to note that it may seem unusual for the court to prefer the evidence of a solicitor to that of an experienced medical practitioner on what appears to be a clinical decision. This was not without precedent, however, and in *Birkin v Wing* (1890) 63 LT 80, for example, the judge preferred the evidence of a solicitor who considered that his client was mentally capable of entering into a particular contract, to that of a doctor who said that he lacked capacity.

Where an expert assessor is required, it is necessary to determine the specific issue or issues for consideration to help identify who is the most appropriate person to instruct to conduct the capacity assessment. Examples include:

- general practitioner

- psychiatrist

- geriatrician

- speech and language therapist
- social worker

General practitioners are often reluctant to prepare a capacity report and, in any case, it is generally preferable for an expert capacity assessor to be instructed. Although this will likely result in a higher financial cost to the client for the report to be carried out, it will usually carry greater weight in any subsequent challenge. It may also provide greater protection to the practitioner.

When instructing a capacity assessor, the practitioner should provide clear instructions which include:

- basic information about the client including any health concerns and diagnoses
- the nature and extent of the expertise required
- the purpose of the report
- the specific issue or issues for consideration
- an explanation of the relevant legal tests, including the burden of proof
- any timescales
- confirmation of costs

A precedent letter of instruction is contained in Appendix 3.

CHAPTER FOUR

WHEN A CAPACITY ASSESSMENT MAY BE REQUIRED

It may not only be in circumstances where the practitioner is concerned as to whether the client lacks capacity to provide instructions where it may be appropriate for a capacity assessment to be obtained. Other situations may include:

- where a lasting power of attorney is being executed and it is likely to give rise to an objection, for example where one child is not being appointed as attorney. Having a capacity assessment from the time the lasting power of attorney was executed, prepared by an expert specifically assessing capacity to make a lasting power of attorney is likely to help mitigate any objection, including the time it takes to resolve, the cost and reducing the likelihood of any court action.

- where the client is making a will which is likely to give rise to a claim, for example where unequal provision is being made for children. A contemporaneous capacity assessment should help mitigate the effect of any claim. This may also be relevant in relation to any potential claim against the firm who prepared the will by the executor and/or beneficiaries (or disappointed beneficiaries).

- *Kenward v Adams* (The Times (29 November 1975)) where Templeman J observed "when a solicitor is drawing up a will for an aged testator or one who has been seriously ill, it should be witnessed or approved by a medical practitioner, who ought to record his examination of the testator and his findings". This is known as the Golden Rule and is discussed later in this book.

- where a client is proposing to make a disposition which will significantly affect their estate and may give rise to claims either during lifetime or on death.

- archiving requests made by attorneys or deputies, particularly where there are potential safeguarding concerns.

CHAPTER FIVE

MENTAL CAPACITY ACT 2005: THE PRINCIPLES

The current legal framework in relation to mental capacity was established by the Mental Capacity Act 2005 ("MCA"). The MCA makes it clear that the definition of lack of capacity and the test of capacity as set out in the MCA are "for the purposes of the Act" and as such, will only apply to decisions covered by the MCA. This is affirmed in the MCA Code of Practice at paragraph 4.33, which states that the statutory definition of capacity is in line with common law tests and the MCA does not replace them. There is some academic debate as to the extent this is correct and so in some circumstances, particularly in relation to wills, it may be necessary to apply the MCA and common law concurrently. However, for the purposes of most legal decisions, it is the MCA test of capacity that will apply.

Section 1 Mental Capacity Act 2005: the principles

All decisions made on behalf of or in respect of a person who lacks capacity must be made pursuant to the principles of the MCA, as set out in section 1. These principles are:

1. A person must be assumed to have capacity unless it is established that he lacks capacity.

2. A person it not to be treated as unable to make a decision unless all practicable steps to help him to do so have been taken without success.

3. A person is not to be treated as unable to make a decision merely because he makes an unwise decision.

4. An act done or decision made under the MCA for or on behalf of a person who lacks capacity must be done, or made, in his best interests.

5. Before the act is done, or the decision is made, regard must be had as to whether the purpose for which it is needed can be as effectively achieved in a way that is less restrictive of the person's rights and freedom of action.

Section 1(2) Mental Capacity Act 2005: presumption of capacity

The MCA creates a rebuttable presumption of capacity, reflecting the common law position (as identified by Kennedy LJ in his Court of Appeal judgment in *Masterman-Lister v Jewell* [2003] 3 All ER 162 where he stated that capacity was a right 'with which no lawyer and no court should rush to interfere").

In practice, where concerns are raised regarding a client's capacity to provide instructions, it may be necessary for a formal assessment of capacity to be carried out, either by the practitioner or by a medical expert. This is covered more below.

The presumption of capacity still applies even where a client has a deputy or attorney appointed and the practitioner will still need to satisfy themselves that the client lacks capacity to take the decision in question. The legal basis for this is that the deputy or attorney only has authority to make a decision on behalf of the client if the client lacks capacity to make the decision for themselves. There is a significant risk to the practitioner if they fail to ascertain the client's capacity. The practitioner's duty is to the client; the deputy or attorney is acting as an agent only. This is covered in further detail later in the book.

Section 1(3) Mental Capacity Act 2005: providing practical support

In addition to the presumption of capacity, section 1 MCA further states that "a person it not to be treated as unable to make a decision unless all practicable steps to help him to do so have been taken without success" (section 1(3) MCA). A practitioner cannot assume that a person lacks capacity to take a particular decision on the basis that they are unable to assimilate, process or communicate their decision making. Consideration should be had as to how a person can be supported to make a decision – in some situations this may be relatively easy, for example using braille for someone with a visual impairment (assuming the person feels comfortable communicating in this way), but in other situations this may be more difficult and require creative thinking. Supportive decision making is a key part of section 1(3) MCA and is considered further below.

Section 1(4) Mental Capacity Act 2005: unwise decisions

Section 1(4) MCA states that "a person is not to be treated as unable to make a decision merely because he makes an unwise decision". The MCA therefore creates a statutory framework designed to preserve a person's "freedom and autonomy" (see *Simpson v Simpson* [1989] Fam Law 20).

It is not unusual for individuals to make decisions that others would not; it is a natural part of human behaviour. It is imperative that the decision maker does not seek to substitute their own views or decision making when considering another's decision. A seemingly unwise decision is not indicative of an incapacitous decision and the individual nature of decision making must be respected.

This principle can be more effectively applied when the decision maker knows more about the individual as a person and whether the proposed decision is in line with the type of decision they would usually make (although as emphasised above, an unusual decision does not mean the person lacks capacity to make the decision in person).

Section 1(5) Mental Capacity Act 2005: best interests

If it has been established that the person to whom the decision relates lacks capacity to take the decision in question, any decision made on behalf of that person must be taken in his or her best interests. Section 4 MCA sets out what constitutes best interests:

"4 Best interests

(1) In determining for the purposes of this Act what is in a person's best interests, the person making the determination must not make it merely on the basis of—

(a) the person's age or appearance, or

(b) a condition of his, or an aspect of his behaviour, which might lead others to make unjustified assumptions about what might be in his best interests.

(2) The person making the determination must consider all the relevant circumstances and, in particular, take the following steps.

(3) He must consider—

(a) whether it is likely that the person will at some time have capacity in relation to the matter in question, and

(b) if it appears likely that he will, when that is likely to be.

(4) He must, so far as reasonably practicable, permit and encourage the person to participate, or to improve his ability to participate, as fully as possible in any act done for him and any decision affecting him.

(5) Where the determination relates to life-sustaining treatment he must not, in considering whether the treatment is in the best interests of the person concerned, be motivated by a desire to bring about his death.

(6) He must consider, so far as is reasonably ascertainable—

(a) the person's past and present wishes and feelings (and, in particular, any relevant written statement made by him when he had capacity)

(b) the beliefs and values that would be likely to influence his decision if he had capacity, and

(c) the other factors that he would be likely to consider if he were able to do so.

(7) He must take into account, if it is practicable and appropriate to consult them, the views of—

(a) anyone named by the person as someone to be consulted on the matter in question or on matters of that kind,

(b) anyone engaged in caring for the person or interested in his welfare,

(c) any donee of a lasting power of attorney granted by the person, and

(d) any deputy appointed for the person by the court

as to what would be in the person's best interests and, in particular, as to the matters mentioned in subsection (6).

(8) The duties imposed by subsections (1) to (7) also apply in relation to the exercise of any powers which—

(a) are exercisable under a lasting power of attorney, or

(b) are exercisable by a person under this Act where he reasonably believes that another person lacks capacity.

(9) In the case of an act done, or a decision made, by a person other than the court, there is sufficient compliance with this section if (having complied with the requirements of subsections (1) to (7)) he reasonably believes that what he does or decides is in the best interests of the person concerned.

(10) "Life-sustaining treatment" means treatment which in the view of a person providing health care for the person concerned is necessary to sustain life.

(11)"Relevant circumstances" are those—

(a) of which the person making the determination is aware, and

(b) which it would be reasonable to regard as relevant".

There is significant case law considering best interests and it will always apply on a matter-by-matter basis. However, some useful general guidance was provided in the cases of *Re G (TJ)* [2010] EWHC 3005 COP and *Re M* (Statutory Will) [2011] 1 WLR 344 which, although both related to statutory will matters, consider at length the general issue of best interests.

In *Re G(TJ)*, Mr Justice Morgan determined that best interests involves a number of factors, including:

- the actual wishes of P

- he beliefs and values which would be likely to influence P's decision

- other factors which P would be likely to consider if he had capacity to do so

- a balance sheet of factors which P would draw up if he had capacity to do so.

Although Mr Justice Morgan accepted that there will be an element of substituted judgment, he emphasised that it is absolutely clear that the ultimate test for the court is the test of best interests and not the test of substituted judgment.

Extending the consideration of best interests, Mr Justice Munby in *Re M* stated:

- there is no hierarchy between the various factors in section 4, that is, the best interests section of the MCA, beyond the overarching principle that what is determinative is the judicial evaluation of what is in P's best interests.

- the weight to be attached to the various section 4 factors will differ depending upon the individual circumstances of the particular case. A feature or factor which in one case may carry great, possibly even preponderant, weight may in another, superficially similar, case carry much less, or even very little, weight.

- there may be one or more features or factors which are of magnetic importance in influencing or even determining the outcome.

- P's wishes and feelings will be a significant factor to which the court must pay close regard. The weight to be attached to those wishes and feelings will always be case specific and fact specific and in considering the weight and importance to be attached to P's wishes and feelings the court must have regard to all the relevant circumstances. These circumstances include:

    1. The degree of P's incapacity.

    2. The strength and consistency of the views expressed by P.

    3. The possible impact on P of knowing that his wishes and feelings have not been given effect to.

    4. The extent to which P's wishes and feelings are, or are not, rational, sensible, responsible and pragmatically capable of implementation.

    5. The extent to which P's wishes and feelings, if given effect, can properly be accommodated within the court's overall assessment of what is in his best interests.

Mr Justice Munby also reiterated that best interests do not cease at the moment of death and this may extend to avoiding post-death litigation. This is particularly relevant when considering post-death arrangements (such as a statutory will).

It is not for the legal practitioner to generally consider best interests or make a judgment over the proposed course of action of an attorney or deputy (see further below where the client is considered to lack capacity), other than potentially raising a safeguarding concern. This concern may be raised with the Office of the Public Guardian, local authority or Police amongst others.

Contact detail for the Office of the Public Guardian's safeguarding team are as follows:

- Office of the Public Guardian
- opg.safeguardingunit@publicguardian.gov.uk
- Telephone: 0115 934 2777
- Textphone: 0115 934 2778
- Monday to Friday, 9:30am to 5pm; Wednesday, 10am to 5pm
- Office of the Public Guardian, PO Box 16185, Birmingham, B2 2WH

Section 1(6) Mental Capacity Act 2005: least restrictive option

The Mental Capacity Act Code of Practice explains the concept of least restrictive option as follows:

"2.14 Before somebody makes a decision or acts on behalf of a person who lacks capacity to make that decision or consent to the act, they must always question if they can do something else that would interfere less with the person's basic rights and freedoms. This is called finding the 'less restrictive alternative'. It includes considering whether there is a need to act or make a decision at all.

2.15 Where there is more than one option, it is important to explore ways that would be less restrictive or allow the most freedom for a person who lacks capacity to make the decision in question. However, the final decision must always allow the original purpose of the decision or act to be achieved.

2.16 Any decision or action must still be in the best interests of the person who lacks capacity. So sometimes it may be necessary to choose an option that is not the least restrictive alternative if that option is in the person's best interests. In practice, the process of choosing a less restrictive option and deciding what is in the person's best interests will be combined. But both principles must be applied each time a decision or action may be taken on behalf of a person who lacks capacity to make the relevant decision".

Mental Capacity Act 2005 principles: summary

1. Presumption of capacity
2. Assist the person to make the decision
3. Cannot treat someone as unable to make a decision because they make an unwise decision
4. Decisions must be taken in the person's best interests
5. Least restrictive option to be taken

CHAPTER SIX

SUPPORTED DECISION MAKING

Over 3 million people in the UK live with conditions which can cause difficulties with decision making. Historically, individuals with impairments which affect their decision-making abilities would have been considered to lack capacity. This attitude is changing, particularly as a result of the UN Convention of the Rights of Persons with Disabilities (CRPD) which has resulted in a number of jurisdictions introducing reforms to legal systems to ensure compliance. It is generally considered that the MCA does not comply with Article 12 CRPD, even with section 1(3) MCA which requires all practicable steps to help the person to make a decision have been taken without success.

Supported decision making is arguably a broader concept than principle 2 MCA (section 1(3) MCA) and is more commonly understood and applied in other jurisdictions. There has been increasing work done in this area and the University of Birmingham's Everyday Decision Research Project is one such example. The report considers ways of supporting individuals with mental impairment to make a will. There have been calls for the MCA Code of Practice to be updated to reflect the broader supported decision taking model. For the time being, chapter 3 of the MCA Code of Practice provides guidance regarding supporting others to make decisions. The guidance includes the following check points:

- Provide relevant information
    - Does the person have all the relevant information they need to make a particular decision
    - If they have a choice, have they been given on all the alternatives

- Communicate in an appropriate way
    - o Could information be explained or presented in a way that is easier of the person to understand
    - o Have different methods of communication been explored if required, including non-verbal communication
    - o Could anyone else help with communication
- Make the person feel at ease
    - o Are there particular times of day when the person's understanding is better
    - o Are there particular locations where they may feel more at ease
    - o Could the decision be put off to see whether the person can make the decision at a later time when circumstances are right for them
- Support the person
    - o Can anyone else help or support the person to make choices or express a view

The guidance then goes on to consider the following:

- How someone can be helped to make a decision
- What information should be provided to people and how it should be provided
    - o What information is relevant
    - o Communication guidance

  - Helping people with specific communication or cognitive problems

- What steps should be taken to put a person at ease
- Timing
- Support from others
- Other ways to enable decision making

CHAPTER SEVEN

MENTAL CAPACITY ACT 2005: TEST OF CAPACITY

The MCA codified the common law test of capacity. The test is contained in sections 2 and 3 MCA.

Section 2 Mental Capacity Act 2005: general test of capacity

The first stage, as set out in section 2(1) MCA, states that "a person lacks capacity in relation to a matter if at the material time, he is unable to make a decision for himself in relation to the matter because of an impairment of, or a disturbance in the functioning of, the mind or brain".

Examples of an impairment or disturbance in the functioning of the mind or brain may include:

- conditions associated with some forms of mental illness
- dementia
- significant learning disabilities
- the long-term effects of brain damage
- physical or medical conditions that cause confusion, drowsiness or loss of consciousness
- delirium
- concussion following a head injury
- the symptoms of alcohol or drug use

It is irrelevant whether the impairment or disturbance is permanent or temporary (section 2(2) MCA) and there does not need to have been any formal diagnosis. Likewise, even where there has been a diagnosis, the practitioner cannot assume the person is unable to take the decision in question.

A lack of capacity cannot be established merely by reference to:

- a person's age or appearance, or
- a condition of his or an aspect of his behaviour, which might lead others to make unjustified assumptions about his capacity (section 2(3) MCA).

In practice, there may be circumstances when a practitioner may become concerned as to a client's capacity, for example if there has been a diagnosis of dementia. These concerns should not be ignored and the practitioner should specifically mention these concerns in their file notes and how those concerns have been alleviated.

The test of capacity is on the balance of probabilities. That is, whether a person is more likely that not to lack capacity to make the decision in question at the particular time (section 2(4) MCA).

Section 3 Mental Capacity Act 2005: functional test of capacity

For the purposes of section 2 MCA, a person is unable to make a decision for himself if he is unable to:

- understand the information relevant to the decision;
- retain that information;
- use or weigh that information as part of the process of making the decision; or
- communicate his decision (whether by talking, using sign language or any other means)

The fact that a person is able to retain the information relevant to a decision for a short period only does not prevent him from being regarded as able to make the decision in question (section 3(3) MCA 2005).

In practice, if a client is unable to retain information for at least part of the meeting, this is going to cause difficulties in obtaining instructions and unless the practitioner is satisfied the client has or lacks capacity to take the decision, it is likely that an expert capacity assessor will need to be instructed unless the practitioner feels confident to state that the client lacks capacity.

Relevant information

Section 3 of the MCA requires the person to understand the information relevant to the decision which includes information about the reasonably foreseeable consequences of deciding one way or another, or failing to make the decision at all (section 3(4) MCA). The relevant information depends on the decision in question and can be determined by reference to case law (see below).

Mental Capacity Act 2005 test of capacity: summary

- At the material time the person has an impairment of, or a disturbance in the functioning of, the mind or brain

- The person needs to:

- understand the information relevant to the decision

- retain that information

- use or weigh that information as part of making the decision

- communicate his decision

CHAPTER EIGHT

SPECIFIC TESTS OF CAPACITY

Capacity to make a lasting power of attorney – *Re Collis* [2010] COP 27/10/10 (unreported)

The test of capacity as set out in the MCA provides the framework in relation to capacity to execute a lasting power of attorney ("LPA"). Relevant information should include information about the consequences of not executing an LPA.

In his judgment in *Re Collis*, Senior Judge Lush considered the difference between capacity needed to make an enduring power of attorney and a lasting power of attorney (lasting powers of attorney were introduced by the Mental Capacity Act 2005 and replaced enduring powers of attorney. Enduring powers of attorney made before 1 October 2007 remain valid but new ones could not be made after that date). The Senior Judge stated "the criteria in Re K, Re F are not entirely applicable to LPAs because of some fairly major differences between EPAs and LPAs, and would need to be adapted in several respects. For example:

- the donor would need to understand that the LPA cannot be used until it is registered by the Public Guardian. This is simply not the case with an EPA.

- one would expect to see a change of emphasis between the creation of an LPA for personal welfare and an LPA for property and affairs; and, in particular, the donor would need to understand that the attorney under an LPA for personal welfare can only make decisions that the donor is contemporaneously incapable of making for him- or herself.

- unlike an EPA, the donor can revoke an LPA at any time when he or she has the capacity to do so (section 19(2)), without the court having to confirm the revocation.

- the authority conferred by an LPA, unlike an EPA, is subject to the provisions of the Mental Capacity Act 2005 and, in particular, sections 1 (the principles) and section 4 (best interests) (section 9(4)).

- the statutory definition of capacity in section 3(4) of the Act specifically requires the donor to be aware of the foreseeable consequences of not executing an LPA, whereas in Re K, Re F Mr Justice Hoffmann did not include an understanding of the effect of not making an EPA in his summary of the matters which should ordinarily be explained to the donor".

As noted above in relation to the professional obligations of legal practitioners, the Senior Judge preferred the contemporaneous evidence of the solicitor who acted as certificate provider when considering the capacity of the donor. A certificate provider is required to confirm that the donor of the LPA at the time the LPA is signed:

- the donor understands the purpose of the LPA and the scope of the authority conferred under it;

- no fraud or undue pressure is being used to induce the donor to create the LPA;

- there is nothing else which would prevent this LPA from being created by the completion of the instrument.

Capacity to manage property and financial affairs – *A, B and C v X, Y* [2012] EWHC 2400 (COP)

In his judgment, Hedley J noted (at 41) "the general concept of managing affairs is an ongoing act and, therefore, quite unlike the specific act of making a will or making an enduring power of attorney. The management of affairs relates to a continuous state of affairs whose demands may be unpredictable and may occasionally be urgent".

Whether someone lacks capacity to manage his property and affairs will depend on the individual circumstances. More complex affairs will require a higher level of mental capacity. It is imperative to differentiate between various decisions to be made and that a client may be able to make some of these decisions, on some occasions, but not others.

Capacity to litigate – *Masterman-Lister v Jewell* [2002] EWCA Civ 1889

In *Masterman-Lister v Jewell,* the Court of Appeal identified the key question as being whether "a party to legal proceedings is capable of understanding, with the assistance of such proper explanation (in broad terms and simple language) from legal advisers and other experts as the case may require, the matter on which their consent or decision was likely to be necessary in the course of those proceedings" (paragraph 75). Furthermore (at paragraph 79), " a person should not be held unable to understand the information relevant to a decision if he can understand and explanation of that information in broad terms and simple language; and that he should not be regarded as unable to make a rational decision merely because the decision which he does, in fact, make is a decision which would not be made by a person on ordinary prudence".

The test applies to the proceedings as a whole and not at each step in the conduct of the proceedings. This was confirmed in *Dunhill v Burgin* [2014] UKSC 18.

As has already been emphasised, capacity is time and matter specific: the litigant must have capacity to conduct the particular proceedings with which they are involved, the ability to conduct other proceedings or make decisions in general is not relevant (*Sheffield City Council v E and another* [2005] Fam 326).

As noted by Mr Justice Mostyn in *Re P* [2021] EWCOP 27, "conducting litigation is not simply a question of providing instructions to a lawyer and the sitting back and watching the case unfold. Litigation is a heavy-duty, dynamic transactional process both prior to and in court, with information to be recalled, instructions to be given, advice to be received and decisions to be taken, on many occasions, on a number of issues, over the span of the proceedings as they develop: *TB and KB v LH (Capacity to Conduct Proceedings)* [2019] EWCOP 14". As such, the level of capacity required to conduct litigation is set relatively high.

Furthermore, Mr Justice Mostyn stated that, in his opinion, a litigant needs the same level of capacity to conduct litigation whether she is represented or not [paragraph 31].

When considering whether a client has capacity to conduct proceedings, consider whether they can:

- understand how the proceedings are to be funded
- understand the possibility of not succeeding and the risk of having to pay costs
- make the types of decisions which arise in litigation
- give proper instructions for, and approve the particulars of a claim, and approve a compromise

For a client to have capacity to agree a compromise, they would need:

- insight into the compromise
- an ability to instruct solicitors to advise them on it
- an understanding of the solicitor's advice
- to be able to weight that advice before making a decision

Capacity to gift – Re *Beaney* [1978] 2 All ER 595

"The degree or extent of understanding required in respect of any instrument is relative to the particular transaction which it is to effect ...

in the case of ... a gift inter vivos ... the degree required varies with the circumstances of the transaction. Thus where at one extreme the subject matter and value of the gift are trivial in relation to the donor's other assets a low degree of understanding will suffice. But, at the other extreme, if its effect is to dispose of the donor's only asset of value and thus ... to pre-empt the devolution of his estate ... then the degree of understanding required is as high as that required for a will, and the donor must understand the claims of all potential donees and the extent of the property to be disposed of" (Sir Martin Nourse QC).

The High Court in *Kicks v Leigh* [2014] EWHC 3926 (Ch) confirmed that the common law test is the correct test.

To engage in social media – *Re A (Capacity: Social Media and Internet Use: Best Interests)* [2019] EWCOP 2 (February 2019)

Mr Justice Cobb determined that the issue as to whether someone has capacity to engage in social media for the purposes on online contact is distinct from the consideration of other forms of direct or indirect contact. He was also satisfied that wider internet use is different to general issues surrounding care. He identified particular characteristics of social media networking and internet use which distinguish it from other forms of contact and care, which include significant scope for harassment, bullying, exposure to harmful content, sexual grooming exploitation (in its many forms), encouragement of self-harm, access to dangerous individuals and/or information.

The relevant information under section 3(1)(a) MCA P needs to be able to understand, retain and use and weigh to be able to make a decision is:

(i) information and images (including videos) which you share on the internet or through social media could be shared more widely, including with people you don't know, without you knowing or being able to stop it;

(ii) it is possible to limit the sharing of personal information or images (and videos) by using 'privacy and location settings' on some internet and social media sites;

(iii) if you place material or images (including videos) on social media sites which are rude or offensive, or share those images, other people might be upset or offended;

(iv) some people you meet or communicate with ('talk to') online, who you don't otherwise know, may not be who they say they are ('they may disguise, or lie about, themselves'); someone who calls themselves a 'friend' on social media may not be friendly;

(v) some people you meet or communicate with ('talk to') on the internet or through social media, who you don't otherwise know, may pose a risk to you; they may lie to you, or exploit or take advantage of you sexually, financially, emotionally and/or physically; they may want to cause you harm;

(vi) if you look at or share extremely rude or offensive images, messages or videos online you may get into trouble with the policy, because you may have committed a crime.

Mr Justice Cobb added the following points to assist in its interpretation and application:

i) in relation to (ii) above, [he did] not envisage that the precise details or mechanisms of the privacy settings need to be understood but P should be capable of understanding that they exist, and be able to decide (with support) whether to apply them;

ii) in relation to (iii) and (vi) above, [Mr Justice Cobb used] the term 'share' in this context as it is used in the 2018 Government Guidance: 'Indecent Images of Children: Guidance for Young People': that is to say. "sending on an email, offering on a file sharing platform, uploading to a site that other people have access to, and possessing with a view to distribute";

iii) in relation to (iii) and (vi) above, [Mr Justice Cobb chose] the words 'rude or offensive' – as these words may be easily understood by those with learning disabilities as including not only the insulting and abusive, but also the sexually explicit, indecent or pornographic;

iv) in relation to (vi) above, this is not intended to represent a statement of the criminal law, but is designed to reflect the importance, which a capacitous person would understand, of not searching for such material, as it may have criminal content, and/or steering away from such material if accidently encountered, rather than investigating further and/or disseminating such material. Counsel in this case cited from the Government Guidance on 'Indecent Images of Children' (see (ii) above). Whilst the Guidance does not refer to 'looking at' illegal images as such, a person should know that entering into this territory is extremely risky and may easily lead a person into a form of offending. This piece of information (in [28](vi)) is obviously more directly relevant to general internet use rather than communications by social media, but it is relevant to social media use as well.

Mr Justice Cobb added that whilst he had considered whether to include the potentially psychologically harmful impact on the user, he took the view that many capacitous internet users do not specifically consider this risk, or if they do, they are indifferent to the risk and he therefore did not think it was appropriate to include it in the list of information relevant to the test of capacity.

To engage in sexual relations – *A Local Authority v JB* (Rev 2) [2020] EWCA Civ 735 (11 June 2020)

Guidance was given by the Court of Appeal in *A Local Authority v JB* as to the information relevant to a decision whether to engage in sexual relations.

"…

100 In summary, when considering whether, as a result of an impairment of, or disturbance in the functioning of, the mind or

brain, a person is unable to understand, retain, or use or weigh information relevant to a decision whether to engage in sexual relations, the information relevant to the decision may include the following:

(1) the sexual nature and character of the act of sexual intercourse, including the mechanics of the act;

(2) the fact that the other person must have the capacity to consent to the sexual activity and must in fact consent before and throughout the sexual activity;

(3) the fact that P can say yes or no to having sexual relations and is able to decide whether to give or withhold consent;

(4) that a reasonably foreseeable consequence of sexual intercourse between a man and woman is that the woman will become pregnant;

(5) that there are health risks involved, particularly the acquisition of sexually transmitted and transmissible infections, and that the risk of sexually transmitted infection can be reduced by the taking of precautions such as the use of a condom.

101 There remains the question whether the information relevant to the decision whether to engage in sexual relations must always include all of the matters identified in the previous paragraph.

102 This is clearly a matter of considerable importance. In NB, Hayden J held that an assessment of the information relevant to a decision to have sexual relations requires the incorporation of P's circumstances and characteristics according to the facts of the particular case. NB was not the first case in which this approach was adopted. As illustrated above, it was an approach I adopted myself in Re TZ when I observed in passing that the relevant information included the risks of pregnancy "if the relations are heterosexual".

103 It is important to note, however, that the question whether the information relevant to the decision whether to engage in sexual relations must always include all of the matters identified in paragraph 100 above does not arise on the present appeal. Any observations we might make on the subject would therefore not be binding authority. The summary of the case law set out above illustrates that on several occasions judicial obiter dicta in this difficult area of the law have been initially followed by other judges, only to be rejected in later cases after hearing further argument. For that reason, it would be prudent for this Court to refrain from commenting until it has an opportunity to hear full argument on the point in a case where the issue arises on the appeal."

Wills

Capacity to make a will

The long-standing test of capacity at common law is that set out in *Banks v Goodfellow* [1870] LR 5 QB 549, the test being that "it is essential to the exercise of such a power [i.e. to make a will] that the testator:

1. shall understand the nature of the act and its effects;

2. shall understand the extent of the property of which he is disposing;

3. shall be capable to comprehend and appreciate the claims to which he ought to give effect; and

4. with a view to the latter object, that no disorder of the mind shall poison his affections, pervert his sense of right, or prevent the exercise of his natural faculties – that no insane delusions shall influence his will in disposing of his property and bring about the disposal of it which, if the mind had been sound, would not have been made".

To these four tests, a fifth was arguably added by Mr Justice Briggs in *Key v Key* [2010] EWHC 408 which extended the *Banks v Goodfellow* test by taking into account the decision-making powers of the testator as a whole.

The *Banks v Goodfellow* test has recently been upheld as the applicable law in *Re Clitheroe* [2021] 1102 (Ch).

There are two primary stages at which capacity is assessed:

1. when instructions are provided (which may be on more than one occasion)

2. when the will is executed

It is possible for the testator's capacity to have deteriorated between providing instructions and executing the will. In *Parker v Felgate* (1883) 8 PD 171, it was established that the test of capacity at the time the will is signed is as follows:

1. when the will is executed, does the testator remember and understand the instructions given to their solicitor?

2. is the testator capable of understanding each clause of the will if it was explained to them?

3. is the testator capable of understanding, and do they understand, that they are executing a will for which they had previously given instructions to their solicitor?

If the answer to any of the questions is yes, the will is valid. This principle has been further applied in cases such as *Clancy v Clancy* [2003] EWHC 1885 (Ch) and *Perrins v Holland* [2010] EWCA Civ 840. It has also been applied in relation to lifetime gifts on the basis the same underlying reasons for the decision apply to lifetime dispositions as well as on death (*Singellos v Singellos* [2010] EWHC 2353 (Ch)).

The MCA does not replace the common law test of capacity to make a will and this was confirmed in a number of post-MCA cases including *Scammell v Farmer* [2008] EWHC 1100 (Ch) and *Walker v Badmin*

[2014] All ER (D) 258 where the judge dealt specially with the issue as to which test of capacity should apply, confirming it was the common law test and not the MCA. The MCA Code of Practice at paragraphs 4.32 and 4.33 confirms that the MCA definition of capacity reflects the common law test and does not replace it. It can, however, be argued that the MCA definition of capacity is wider than that in *Banks v Goodfellow*.

A person's capacity to make a will must be considered as a distinct decision and it is possible that a client may lack capacity to manage their property and affairs but does have capacity to make a will (see *A, B and C v X, Y* [2012] EWHC 2400 (COP)).

The Golden Rule

As discussed earlier in this book, the Golden Rule relates to cases or an aged testator or one who has suffered a serious illness. It was established by Templeman J in *Kenward v Adams* [1975] CLY 359 and defined in *Re Simpson* [1977] 121 SJ 224 as:

"This 'rule' should always be observed, however straightforward matters may appear and however difficult or tactless it may be to suggest that precaution be taken. The making of a will by such a testator ought to be witnessed or approved by a medical practitioner who satisfied himself of the capacity and understanding of the testator, and records and preserves his examination and finding."

The Golden Rule has been confirmed in subsequent case law, including in *Key v Key* where the draftsman was criticised for not following it: "a significant element of responsibility for this tragic state of affairs lies with the draftsman".

However, failure to observe the Golden Rule does not invalidate the will (see *Scammell v Farmer*) and nor does non-compliance demonstrate its invalidity (for example in *Key v Key*) and *Todd v Parsons and Others* [2019] EWHC 3366 (Ch) where it was stated that the Golden Rule was not "a touchstone of validity"). Compliance should, however, assist with avoiding retrospective questions about testamentary capacity, although this does not preclude a challenge to capacity from being raised.

There may be circumstances when it is difficult to comply with the Golden Rule. For example, in *Wharton v Bancroft* [2011] EWHC 3250 (Ch), Norris J noted (obiter) that in the situation where a solicitor is instructed to prepare a death-bed will, it may not be possible for the solicitor to "simply conjure up a medical attendant". See also *Re S* [2010] EWHC 2405 (COP) and *Hawes v Burgess* [2013] EWCA Civ 74 where a solicitor's attendance note was preferred to retrospective evidence from a medical expert.

Presumption of testamentary capacity

The common law position is that there is a presumption of capacity in relation to a will where it is duly executed and appears rational on the face of it (*Ledger v Wootton* [2007] EWHC 90 (Ch)) and the evidential burden is on the objector to raise a real doubt about capacity. Where a real doubt is raised, the burden shifts to the person or persons asserting the testator did have capacity.

The MCA establishes a presumption of capacity and it has been argued that this changes the common law position insofar as it places the burden on the party questioning capacity to establish that the person lacks capacity, rather than to raise a real doubt.

In *Scammell v Farmer* it was noted that there is an obvious difference between the position at common law and the MCA in that the onus of proof of incapacity under section 1(2) MCA "is from the outset and remains on the complainant which differs from the common law position".

Revocation of a will

The testamentary test of capacity to make a will (as set out in *Banks v Goodfellow*) also applies to the revocation of a will (see *Re Sabatini* [1969] 114 SJ 35).

Capacity to agree legal costs: *ACC & Ors (property and affairs deputy; recovering assets costs for legal proceedings)* [2020] EWCOP 9)

If a client has capacity to give instructions, they will also have capacity to agree the costs (see paragraph 59.1 of Senior Judge Hilder's judgment in *ACC & Ors (property and affairs deputy; recovering assets costs for legal proceedings).*

Remote capacity assessments and use of technology

Remote capacity assessments bring their own challenges. However, the underlying good practice framework still applies including meeting the client alone, applying the relevant test of capacity and keeping detailed attendance notes. Remember, the client may be unfamiliar with communicating through video and it may take a little longer for them to become comfortable to do so. Consider using online tools, such as sharing screens, to give power to the client to write, draw or share their screen. This can help support a client with decision making and can also help with forming an opinion as to a client's understanding and ultimately, their capacity to take the decision in question.

Subject to obtaining the client's consent, the practitioner may wish to record meetings (video or voice record) and keep a record with the client's papers. This may assist with any subsequent challenge to the will or the circumstances regarding the signing of it.

Where an expert capacity assessor is instructed, they should be able to complete the capacity assessment virtually if required.

Wherever possible, a capacity assessment should take place in person. Where it is necessary to conduct a virtual capacity assessment, the practitioner should consider ways in which the potential risks can be mitigated. This may include compliance with good practice (as set out above), meeting the person on more than one occasion and potentially at different times or locations (although remember that capacity is time and matter specific).

CHAPTER NINE

ASSESSMENT OF CAPACITY

Steps to assessing capacity

It can be useful to establish and apply a common form of capacity assessment for all clients, regardless as to whether there are concerns over their capacity. Using a precedent form will help to mitigate mistakenly not applying part of the assessment, will act as a basis of an attendance note and will be available in the future should any queries over a person's capacity arise (this may be in relation to later wills and any earlier capacity assessment can help build a picture of the client's historic capacity, wishes and instructions). The following format is suggested:

1. Identify the decision to be made (for example, whether the client has capacity to make a lasting power of attorney).

2. Identify the legal test to be applied (for example, the MCA)

3. Consider what is relevant information (for example in relation to lasting powers of attorney, the information set out in *Re Collis* [2010] COP 27/10/10 (unreported) and considering issues such as who the proposed attorneys are, why they are appropriate, what kind of decisions will they be able to make etc).

4. Identify any additional support the client may need (for example, more than one meeting, seeing the client at home, using a picture board etc).

5. Record the meeting fully, including the questions asked and responses received. This should be done contemporaneously.

Case studies applying these steps are considered further below.

Practical tips

For practitioners unfamiliar or uncomfortable with assessing capacity on a regular basis, it can be a daunting process. The following tips should help.

1. Understand the person. This helps to build trust with the client, understand their wishes and feelings (which will be relevant if a section 4 MCA best interests decision is required) and build a broader picture of the consistency and rationality of the client's answers.

2. Understand the person's injury or illness, how it may affect the decision-making process and what some of the symptoms may be. The practitioner will need to be mindful and may need to suggest another meeting on another day or location.

3. Work with other professionals who may know the person better than the practitioner, or parts of the person's life better than the practitioner. Examples may be social workers or care workers.

4. Identify whether there are any tools available to assist with decision making. For example, communication tools such as eye gaze, Makaton or pictures, financial planning and budgeting tools such as Goodbudget, Clio or cash cards, or other tools which help to promote independence such as Siri.

5. Be patient. It may be necessary to hold more than one meeting with the client in order to properly assess capacity. The client must not be pressured to make a decision when they are not ready to do so.

6. Apply a risk-based approach. For example, if there is a risk of a challenge to capacity, even if it is felt the client has capacity to take the particular decision, obtain a medical report (subject to obtaining the client's consent).

In *JKS and ADS v DSM* [2017] EWCOP 8, Charles J provided guidance to those undertaking capacity assessments and stated the following should be considered:

i. P was seen in circumstances that would reduce family influences (such as a neutral venue and at least not in the presence of family members);

ii. The history they took and were given is balanced, applied with care and in a way that recognised the difference between fact and assertion; and

iii. The explanations, questions and prompts given to P were appropriately framed (e.g. as to why P was expressing the views that he/she was and what P remembered about relevant parts of his/her family history).

Tips for assessing capacity: summary

1. Understand the person
2. Understand the person's injury or illness, how it may affect the decision-making process and what some of the symptoms may be
3. Identify whether there are any tools available to assist with decision making
4. Be patient
5. See the client alone
6. Ask relevant questions
7. Apply a risk-based approach. If in doubt, obtain a formal capacity assessment.

Questioning techniques

1. Use simple language.

2. Consider using different forms of communication such as pictures.

3. Ask general questions. This helps to facilitate trust and rapport and will also assist the practitioner to begin considering whether the client is providing consistent and rational answers. Such questions can be a mix of open and closed questions.

4. Come back to some questions as a way of checking the consistency and accuracy of the client's answers.

5. Ask the client to confirm what their understanding of the purpose of the meeting is and any agreed instructions. Family members will often be the ones to arrange the meeting but the client may not know the purpose of the meeting when you meet with them.

6. Ask the client to confirm their understanding of the advice you provide.

7. The practitioner must identify the relevant information and build their questions around it. They should prepare the questions in advance, although be ready to ask follow up questions if necessary. Examples of questions may include (in relation to the sale of property):

    a. what is the address of your property

    b. when did you move there

    c. what is the sale price. The client may not need to know this exactly but should have a broad idea.

    d. what could you buy for (say) £300,000

    e. where will you live

   f. if the client is buying a replacement property, what are they going to do with any excess sale proceeds

8. The practitioner needs to know the answers to as many of the questions as possible. Just because a client's answers appear rational (or irrational), it does not mean they are correct.

9. Do the answers feel right? Sometimes gut instinct can be very powerful.

10. What is the risk. If in doubt, obtain a capacity assessment.

Attendance notes

The significance and importance of an attendance note cannot be overstated. A good attendance note should include (but is not limited to):

- personal details of the client (name, address, age, any health conditions or injuries)

- details of assets and liabilities, including how they are held where ownership is joint

- details of the client's family and dependants

- the questions asked and answers received – these should be verbatim where possible

- details of the advice given

- who was present at the meeting (the practitioner must, wherever possible, ensure they meet with the client alone for at least part of the meeting)

- assessment of capacity. This should record

    - the decision to be made

  - the legal test

  - the relevant law (for example, the MCA, Banks v Goodfellow)

  - how each part of the test was satisfied

- next steps agreed

The practitioner should consider asking the client to sign a copy of the attendance note confirming it is an accurate reflection of the meeting. They may also wish to consider making a video recording of the meeting (with the client's consent).

A precedent attendance note can be found in Appendix 2.

CHAPTER TEN

RETROSPECTIVE ASSESSMENTS

It is possible for retrospective capacity assessments to be carried out, although they will not be as accurate as a contemporaneous assessment. The person assessing capacity will need to form an overall picture of the person and may use some or all of the following to assist with this:

- medical records
- health and social care notes (perhaps kept by the local authority, care agency or care home)
- previous capacity assessments
- professional records
- family and friends

Any retrospective assessment will be carried out in accordance with the appropriate legal framework (for example, the Mental Capacity Act 2005) and to the civil standard of proof (balance of probabilities).

Where there are concerns that an allegation of a lack of capacity may arise in the future, it may be worth considering arranging a contemporaneous assessment of capacity to be carried out, even where the practitioner does not have current concerns over the client's capacity. This is on the basis that a capacity assessment carried out at the time of the decision being made will be preferred to a retrospective assessment and may help to 1) mitigate a future claim and 2) enable any claim or challenge to be dealt with as quickly and efficiently as possible.

In addition to a formal assessment of capacity, it may be beneficial for other evidence to be obtained and retained. Examples may be for the person to regularly review (and document) their will (preferably through a legal practitioner), videos of the person interacting and engaging with others (not necessarily in relation to legal activities), written evidence of the person and ensuring that health and social care records are sufficiently detailed.

As noted earlier in this book, although a retrospective assessment should be carried out by an expert, such as a psycho-geriatrician, wherever possible, the court may consider that a contemporaneous attendance note, even if not from a medical practitioner, may be preferable to a retrospective expert assessment (*Re Collis* [2010] COP 27/10/10 (unreported)).

CHAPTER ELEVEN

CHALLENGING CAPACITY ASSESSMENTS

It is ultimately a judicial decision as to whether a person has or lacks capacity (*Richmond v Richmond* [1914] 111 LT 273). Where there is dispute, the practitioner may wish to consider making an application to the Court of Protection to ask the court to make a declaration pursuant to section 15 MCA 2005. Unless proceedings are already ongoing in the Court of Protection, a new application will need to be made using form COP1 (application form) and COP24. Other supplementary forms may be required, depending on who is making the application and the background issues.

The cost of making an application to the Court of Protection can be significant and it is likely to take some time for a decision to be made. In the first instance, consider instructing a second (or even third) expert. If the expert is required as part of litigation proceedings, it may be appropriate for each side to agree to instruct their own choice of expert (subject to the client's consent).

CHAPTER TWELVE

VULNERABILITY FACTORS

There may be circumstances in which a client has capacity to provide instructions but there are still concerns over vulnerability. There are three broad categories of vulnerable client:

1. clients who have capacity to make decisions and provide instructions but require additional support

2. clients who lack capacity to make decisions and provide instructions

3. clients who are vulnerable to undue influences

There are various regulatory and legislative obligations with regard to such clients and the failure of a legal practitioner to meet the professional duties within the SRA's Code of Conduct for Solicitors may result in SRA sanctions or a referral to the Solicitors' Disciplinary Tribunal. There may also be a referral to the Legal Ombudsman or a discrimination claim for failure to make reasonable adjustments under the Equality Act 2010.

Indicators of vulnerability include:

- age

- physical disabilities

- learning disabilities

- brain injury

- long-term alcohol or drug use

- psychological or emotional factors

- developmental disability

Practitioners must identify the client's needs and they should do this by ascertaining from the client whether they:

- have any needs or preferences for communicating with the practitioner

- need assistance to access services

- need assistance for how services are provided

- are able to understand and action information and advice provided

It is good practice for a firm to have a vulnerable client policy – and to be shared with staff. Some professional accreditation schemes, such as the Law Society's Wills and Inheritance Quality Scheme, require firms to identify the needs of vulnerable clients and the best way to record these are in a firm wide policy.

CHAPTER THIRTEEN

CASE STUDIES

These are not intended to be a comprehensive set of examples, particularly the suggested questions to be asked, but they provide a broad summary of the issues and the questions to be considered.

Lasting powers of attorney

DECISION TO BE MADE	Whether the donor has capacity to make a gift
LEGAL TEST	Sections 2 and 3 Mental Capacity Act 2005: - a person lacks capacity in relation to a matter if at the material time, he is unable to make a decision for himself in relation to the matter because of an impairment of, or a disturbance in the functioning of, the mind or brain - The person must: o understand the information relevant to the decision; o retain that information; o use or weigh that information as part of the process of making the decision; or

	○ communicate his decision (whether by talking, using sign language or any other means)
RELEVANT INFORMATION	*Re Collis* [2010] COP 27/10/10 (unreported)
EXAMPLE QUESTIONS TO ASK	- what is a power of attorney - what types of decisions will your attorneys be able to make - who are your proposed attorneys - what relationship to you are your attorneys - why have you chosen them to act as your attorneys - when may you need a power of attorney - why do you want to make a lasting power of attorney - what is the nature and scope of the powers you are giving your attorneys

Gifts

<table>
<tr><td>DECISION TO BE MADE</td><td>Whether the donor has capacity to make a lasting power of attorney</td></tr>
<tr><td>LEGAL TEST</td><td>Sections 2 and 3 Mental Capacity Act 2005:

- a person lacks capacity in relation to a matter if at the material time, he is unable to make a decision for himself in relation to the matter because of an impairment of, or a disturbance in the functioning of, the mind or brain

- The person must:

o understand the information relevant to the decision;

o retain that information;

o use or weigh that information as part of the process of making the decision; or

o communicate his decision (whether by talking, using sign language or any other means)</td></tr>
<tr><td>RELEVANT INFORMATION</td><td>Re Beaney [1978] 2 All ER 595</td></tr>
<tr><td>EXAMPLE QUESTIONS TO ASK</td><td>- what is a power of attorney</td></tr>
</table>

	- what types of decisions will your attorneys be able to make - who are your proposed attorneys - what relationship to you are your attorneys - when may you need a power of attorney

Wills

DECISION TO BE MADE	Whether the donor has capacity to make a will
LEGAL TEST	*Banks v Goodfellow* [1870] LR 5 QB 549 - The testator: o shall understand the nature of the act and its effects; o shall understand the extent of the property of which he is disposing; o shall be capable to comprehend and appreciate the claims to which he ought to give effect; and o with a view to the latter object, that no disorder of the mind shall poison his affections,

	pervert his sense of right, or prevent the exercise of his natural faculties – that no insane delusions shall influence his will in disposing of his property and bring about the disposal of it which, if the mind had been sound, would not have been made".
RELEVANT INFORMATION	*Banks v Goodfellow [1870] LR 5 QB 549*
EXAMPLE QUESTIONS TO ASK	- what is a will - who are your proposed executors - what is the role of an executor - what are your assets - tell me about your family - do you maintain anyone financially - how much would you like to gift to X - what relation are these people to you - what proportion of your estate does this represent

Selling a property

DECISION TO BE MADE	Whether the donor has capacity to sell their property
LEGAL TEST	Sections 2 and 3 Mental Capacity Act 2005: - a person lacks capacity in relation to a matter if at the material time, he is unable to make a decision for himself in relation to the matter because of an impairment of, or a disturbance in the functioning of, the mind or brain - The person must: o understand the information relevant to the decision; o retain that information; o use or weigh that information as part of the process of making the decision; or o communicate his decision (whether by talking, using sign language or any other means)

RELEVANT INFORMATION	*No specific identified case law*
EXAMPLE QUESTIONS TO ASK	- what is the address of your property - when did you move there - why are you selling it - what is the sale price. The client may not need to know this exactly but should have a broad idea. - what could you buy for (say) £300,000 - where will you live - if the client is buying a replacement property, what are they going to do with any excess sale proceeds

PART TWO

PRACTICAL GUIDANCE

CHAPTER FOURTEEN

LACK OF CAPACITY

If it is established the client lacks capacity to provide instructions, it may be possible to take instructions from a third party.

Powers of attorney

A power of attorney is a document by which one party ("the donor") gives to another the authority to act on his behalf and in his own name.

There are many types of power of attorney. Enduring powers of attorney (EPAs) and lasting powers of attorney (LPAs) continue beyond a loss of mental incapacity and can usually be used before the onset of incapacity. General powers of attorney cease to have effect if the donor loses capacity.

Enduring powers of attorney

Since 1 October 2007, it is no longer possible to make an EPA, although existing EPAs will continue to be valid. They cover property and financial affairs only and can be used before a loss of mental capacity, subject to any restrictions in the EPA, and on the direct authority of the donor. They must be registered with the Office of the Public Guardian if the donor has lost or is losing mental capacity to manage their property and financial affairs. If the EPA is unregistered, the practitioner must take your instructions from the donor. If it is registered, it is possible to take instructions from the attorney(s) but the practitioner should consider still consulting with the donor and in particular seek confirmation from the donor that they consent to the practitioner taking instructions from the attorneys. This position is different to that of lasting powers of attorney (see below) as 1) a registered lasting power of attorney is not indicative of a loss of capacity and 2) the rules around EPAs provide for third parties to rely on the existence of a registered EPA.

Is the EPA registered?	**Who can the practitioner take instructions from?**
No	The donor
Yes	The attorney or the donor if they have capacity to take the decision in question

Lasting powers of attorney

There are two types of lasting power of attorney: property & financial affairs and health & welfare. LPAs must be registered with the Office of the Public Guardian before they can be used. Once registered (an subject to any restrictions in the LPA), attorneys can only act on the direct authority of the donor or if the donor lacks mental capacity to take the decision in question, in the best interests of the donor (see section 4 MCA). The practitioner must take your instructions from the donor, where they retain capacity, or the attorney(s), if the donor lacks capacity but as with EPAs, the practitioner should seek specific confirmation from the donor that they consent to this.

Does the donor retain capacity	**Who can the practitioner take instructions from?**
Yes	The donor
No	The attorney but the practitioner will need to satisfy themselves that the donor lacks capacity to take the decision in question (this may be following a capacity assessment carried out by the practitioner or on production of a capacity assessment)

Court of Protection

The Court of a Protection is a distinct court, established by section 45 of the MCA. It may only make decisions on behalf of someone who lacks capacity or in relation to such a person (known as "P") although in *United Lincolnshire Hospitals NHS Trust v CD* [2019] EWCOP 24 (04 July 2019) the court determined that it has, in exceptional circumstances, the power to make an anticipatory declaration of lawfulness, contingent on P losing capacity, pursuant to section 15(1)(c) MCA.

Powers of the Court of Protection

Under sections 15 and 16 of the MCA, the court may:

- make a declaration as to a person's capacity to make a decision;
- make a declaration that a particular act done in relation to a person who lacks capacity is lawful;
- make a decision on behalf of a person who lacks capacity; or
- appoint a deputy to make decisions on behalf of a person who lacks capacity to make those decisions.

The court's principal powers in respect of P's health and welfare are contained in section 17 MCA and in respect of property and financial affairs, section 18 and Schedule 2 MCA.

All the powers set out in sections 17 and 18 MCA can be delegated to a deputy apart from the powers which are expressly reserved to the court and set out in section 20 MCA, for example, creating a settlement or exercising a trustee power (sections 27-29 and 62 MCA).

Authority of attorneys and deputies

The practitioner must check the terms of the Court of Protection order or power of attorney to ensure they are receiving instructions from an authorised party and what is being proposed is within the authority of that party.

Attorneys and deputies can be appointed to act:

- solely
- jointly
- jointly and severally
- under a LPA or as a deputy, jointly for some matters and jointly and severally for others

Where the appointment is joint, the practitioner must obtain instructions from all attorneys or deputies. If one has died or lost capacity, the power of attorney or deputyship order will fail. Where the appointment is joint and several, it is best practice to take instructions from all attorneys or deputies

CHAPTER FIFTEEN

WHO IS THE CLIENT?

Where the client has capacity: the client (even if acting through an attorney). The letter of engagement should be addressed to and signed by the client (and the attorney(s)).

Where the client lacks capacity, the client is still the client. The letter of engagement should be addressed to and signed by the attorney(s) or deputy but the letter of engagement must be clear that the client is the donor (where there is a power of attorney) or P (where there is a deputyship order).

This also applies to archiving requests.

The duty of care of a legal practitioner is to the client. Attorneys and deputies act as agents only. The relationship between agent and principal (and therefore between deputy/attorney and P/donor) carries with it fiduciary duties. If a deputy or attorney acts outside the authorisations of the deputyship order or power of attorney, he is in breach of his duties and acts at personal risk as to costs.

Does the client have capacity to provide instructions?	
Yes	Letter of engagement is addressed to the client
No	Letter of engagement is addressed to the attorney/deputy "as [attorney][deputy] for [name of client]"

CHAPTER SIXTEEN

LACK OF CAPACITY – NEXT STEPS

The next section is designed to provide practical assistance to practitioners if it is established the client lacks capacity to provide instructions and there is no one authorised to act on their behalf.

Acting as a trustee

A deputy cannot exercise trustee powers (section 20(3)(c) MCA 2005) and an attorney acting under an enduring power of attorney or lasting power of attorney can only exercise trustee powers in limited circumstances (principally only in relation land).

Where a trustee lacks capacity to act in that capacity, the process to remove them, and potentially replace them, will depend on a number of factors.

<u>P has the power to appoint and/or retire trustees under the settlement or their consent is required – section 18(1)(j) MCA 2005</u>

The starting point will be to consider whether the trust instrument contains any express provisions as to what is to happen if a trustee lacks capacity. Where the power of appointment and/or retirement is with the incapacitated trustee, an order of the Court of Protection will usually be required pursuant to section 18 MCA 2005 (who will also make consequential vesting or other orders).

<u>Removal of an incapacitated trustee where no replacement required – section 39 Trustee Act 1925</u>

Section 39 Trustee Act 1925 states "where a trustee is desirous of being discharged from the trust, and after his discharge there will be either a trust corporation or at least two to act as trustees to perform the trust,

then, if such trustee as aforesaid by deed declares that he is desirous of being discharged from the trust, and if his co-trustees and such other person, if any, as is empowered to appoint trustees, by deed consent to the discharge of the trustee, and to the vesting in the co-trustees alone of the trust property, the trustee desirous of being discharged shall be deemed to have retired from the trust, and shall, by the deed, be discharged therefrom under this Act, without any new trustee being appointed in his place".

As such, where an incapacitated trustee does not need to be replaced, an application can be made to the Court of Protection to exercise P's right to retire and be discharged from the trust pursuant to section 39 Trustee Act 1925. The application will be for "the deputy to be authorised in the name and on behalf of P to exercise the power vested in P of retiring from the trusts [as described] and for such purpose to execute such deeds as may be necessary".

Where P is a trustee with a beneficial interest and there is another trustee – section 36(9) Trustee Act 1925

Section 36(9) Trustee Act 1925 states "where a trustee lacks capacity to exercise his functions as trustee and is also entitled in possession to some beneficial interest in the trust property, no appointment of a new trustee in his place shall be made by virtue of paragraph (b) of subsection (1) of this section unless leave to make the appointment has been given by the Court of Protection".

In these circumstances, an application will need to be made to the Court of Protection to obtain authority for the remaining trustee(s) to appoint a new trustee(s). The process is set out below.

Where P is a trustee without a beneficial interest and there is a remaining competent trustee(s) – section 36(1) Trustee Act 1925

Section 36(1) Trustee Act 1925 sets out the circumstances in which a trustee "either original or substituted, and whether appointed by a court or otherwise, is dead, or remains out of the United Kingdom for more than twelve months, or desires to be discharged from all or any of the trusts or powers reposed in or conferred on him, or refuses or is unfit to act therein, or is incapable of acting therein, or is an infant, then, subject to the restrictions imposed by this Act on the number of trustees,—

(a) the person or persons nominated for the purpose of appointing new trustees by the instrument, if any, creating the trust; or

(b) if there is no such person, or no such person able and willing to act, then the surviving or continuing trustees or trustee for the time being, or the personal representatives of the last surviving or continuing trustee;

may, by writing, appoint one or more other persons (whether or not being the persons exercising the power) to be a trustee or trustees in the place of the trustee so deceased remaining out of the United Kingdom, desiring to be discharged, refusing, or being unfit or being incapable, or being an infant, as aforesaid".

As such, where P is a trustee but without a beneficial interest in the trust, it may be possible for the remaining trustees to appoint a new trustee or trustees pursuant to section 36(1) Trustee Act 1925 in place of the incapacitated trustee. This would usually be exercised by way of deed. A precedent is contained in Appendix 5.

Where P is a trustee without a beneficial interest and no remaining competent trustee(s) – section 41 Trustee Act 1925

Where sections 36(1) or 36(9) Trustee Act 1925 do not apply, an application can be made to the Chancery Division of the High Court to appoint a new trustee or trustees pursuant to section 41 Trustee Act 1925.

Section 41 allows the court to appoint a new trustee or trustees when "it is found inexpedient difficult or impracticable so to do without the assistance of the court". As section 41 does not automatically vest the trust assets in the new trustee(s), an application pursuant to section 54 Trustee Act 1925 may be more appropriate (see below).

Where P is a trustee without a beneficial interest and no remaining competent trustee(s) – section 20 Trusts of Land and Appointment of Trustees Act 1986

Section 20 of the Trusts of Land and Appointment of Trustees Act 1986 enables (adult and capacitous) beneficiaries to provide a written direction to appoint a trustee in place of an incapacitated trustee. It provides as follows:

"20 Appointment of substitute for trustee who lacks capacity

(1) This section applies where—

(a) a trustee lacks capacity (within the meaning of the Mental Capacity Act 2005) to exercise] his functions as trustee,

(b) there is no person who is both entitled and willing and able to appoint a trustee in place of him under section 36(1) of the Trustee Act 1925, and

(c) the beneficiaries under the trust are of full age and capacity and (taken together) are absolutely entitled to the property subject to the trust.

(2) The beneficiaries may give to—

(a) a deputy appointed for the trustee by the Court of Protection,

(b) an attorney acting for him under the authority of an enduring power of attorney or lasting power of attorney registered under the Mental Capacity Act 2005

(c) a person authorised for the purpose by the Court of Protection, a written direction to appoint by writing the person or persons specified in the direction to be a trustee or trustees in place of the incapable trustee".

Application where no capable trustee and/or vesting required – section 54 Trustee Act 1925

Where there is no continuing trustee able to appoint or apply for appointment of a new trustee or where a vesting order is required, an application must be made to the Court of Protection for it to exercise its statutory powers pursuant to section 54 of the Trustee Act 1925. This would commonly be required where all legal owners of land lack capacity and replacement trustees are required. In this situation, an application for a deputy for each person must also be being made if a deputy has not already been appointed.

Section 54 Trustee Act 1925 states:

> "(1) Subject to subsection (2), the Court of Protection may not make an order, or give a direction or authority, in relation to a person who lacks capacity to exercise his functions as trustee, if the High Court may make an order to that effect under this Act.
>
> (2) Where a person lacks capacity to exercise his functions as a trustee and a deputy is appointed for him by the Court of Protection or an application for the appointment of a deputy has been made but not determined, then, except as respects a trust which is subject to an order for administration made by the High Court, the Court of Protection shall have concurrent jurisdiction with the High Court in relation to—
>
> (a) mortgaged property of which has become a trustee merely by reason of the mortgage having been paid off;
>
> (b) matters consequent on the making of provision by the Court of Protection for the exercise of a power of appointing trustees or retiring from a trust;
>
> (c) matters consequent on the making of provision by the Court of Protection for the carrying out of any contract entered into by the person concerned;

(d) property to some interest in which the person concerned is beneficially entitled but which, or some interest in which, is held by the person concerned under an express, implied or constructive trust.

The Lord Chancellor may make rules with respect to the exercise of the jurisdiction referred to in this subsection.

Trusts of land

A trust of land exists where there are two or more legal owners of property or where the legal and beneficial owners are different. In this situation, the legal and equitable interests are separated; the legal owner(s) hold the equitable interest on trust for those beneficially entitled. It is only possible for the legal title to be held as joint tenants – no severance is possible, unlike the position with the equitable interest (section 36 Law of Property Act 1925). As such, where one legal owner dies, the legal title will pass by survivorship to the remaining legal owner(s) but their estate may still have a beneficial interest if the equitable interest was held as tenants in common.

Difficulties can arise when one or more of the legal owners lacks capacity to act as a property trustee. In this situation, the process as to how to deal with the land will depend principally on three factors:

1. whether the incapable trustee has a registered enduring power of attorney or lasting power of attorney

2. whether the incapable trustee has a beneficial interest in the land

3. whether there is another competent trustee

Where P is a trustee with a beneficial interest in land and has an attorney (section 1(1) Trustee Delegation Act 1999)

If the incapable trustee has a registered enduring power of attorney (providing 1) it was dated after 29 February 2000, 2) it was dated before 1 March 2000 but it was registered before 1 March 2001 or 3) if an application made to the court for registration of the power before 1

March 2001 has not been finally refused) or a registered lasting power of attorney, and subject to any contrary restrictions in the document itself, and has a beneficial interest in the land, it will be possible for the attorney to exercise a trustee function (section 1 Trustee Delegation Act 1999).

The Trustee Delegation Act 1999 will not assist if P has no interest in the land or where there is no land.

Sole surviving trustee

For dispositions dated after 29 February 2000, section 7 Trustee Delegation Act 1999 provides that a receipt for capital money will overreach beneficial interests only if an attorney acts with at least one other person. Where there is a sole or sole surviving registered proprietor with a Form A restriction in the register and a transfer is executed by their joint attorneys, although two (or more) attorneys have executed the transfer they are considered to be one entity. As such, the transfer is therefore still effectively by a sole proprietor and is caught by the Form A restriction, and the overreaching provisions of the Law of Property Act 1925 are not satisfied.

In this situation, the transfer may be executed by another attorney for the donor (if one has been appointed jointly and severally) or, where the power has been registered, by an additional trustee appointed either by the other joint proprietor or by the attorney under section 8 Trustee Delegation Act 1999.

Section 8 Trustee Delegation Act 1999 (as incorporated in section 36 Trustee Act 1925) enables an attorney to appoint another trustee (and therefore satisfy the overreaching provisions) where both of the following apply:

- A person who is either—

    (a) both a trustee and attorney for the other trustee (if one other), or for both of the other trustees (if two others), under a registered power; or

(b) attorney under a registered power for the trustee (if one) or for both or each of the trustees (if two or three), may, if subsection (6B) of this section is satisfied in relation to him, make an appointment under subsection (6)(b) of this section on behalf of the trustee or trustees (section 36(6A) Trustee Act 1925).

- This subsection is satisfied in relation to an attorney under a registered power for one or more trustees if (as attorney under the power)—

  (e) he intends to exercise any function of the trustee or trustees by virtue of section 1(1) of the Trustee Delegation Act 1999; or

  (f) he intends to exercise any function of the trustee or trustees in relation to any land, capital proceeds of a conveyance of land or income from land by virtue of its delegation to him under section 25 of this Act or the instrument (if any) creating the trust (section 26(6B) Trustee Act 1925).

The appointment can be made in the transfer itself or by separate deed.

Confirmation of beneficial interest

Where the transfer is being signed by the attorney, it is necessary for the attorney to provide a written statement within 2 months of the date of the document confirming that the donor had a beneficial interest in the property (section 2(2) of the Trustee Delegation Act 1999).

The written statement can be made separately if it is dated within 3 months of the date of the document or alternatively, and perhaps most conveniently, the written statement can be included in the disposition itself (in the additional provisions panel of a TR1 or other prescribed form, or in the body of a lease or charge):

"(Name of attorney) confirms that (donor of the power) has a beneficial interest in the property at the date of this (transfer, charge and so on)"

Alternatively, the attorney may adapt the attestation clause as follows:

"Signed as a deed by (name of donor of the power), who has a beneficial interest in the property at the date of this (transfer, charge and so on), acting by their attorney (name of attorney) in the presence of …"

Or the attorney may expand the words of signature as follows:

"John Smith by his attorney Jane Brown who confirms that the donor has a beneficial interest in the property at the date hereof."

If the attorney cannot produce such a statement, HM Land Registry will consider other evidence that the donor had a beneficial interest at the relevant time. A statutory declaration or statement of truth (see practice guide 73: statements of truth) to that effect by a responsible person with full knowledge of the facts may be acceptable in some cases.

<u>Vesting – section 40 Trustee Act 1925</u>

Trust property does not automatically vest in new trustees, even if the appointment is made by deed. Section 40(4) Trustee Act 1925 specifically states automatic vesting does not apply in the following situations:

(a) to land conveyed by way of mortgage for securing money subject to the trust, except land conveyed on trust for securing debentures or debenture stock;

(b) to land held under a lease which contains any covenant, condition or agreement against assignment or disposing of the land without licence or consent, unless, prior to the execution of the deed containing expressly or impliedly the vesting declaration, the requisite licence or consent has been obtained, or unless, by virtue of any statute or rule of law, the vesting declaration, express or implied, would not operate as a breach of covenant or give rise to a forfeiture;

(c) to any share, stock, annuity or property which is only transferable in books kept by a company or other body, or in manner directed by or under an Act of Parliament.

In these situations, a vesting order will be required to transfer the legal title to the new trustee(s) and an application pursuant to section 54 Trustee Act 1925 will need to be made. Section 36 Trustee Act 1925 will not assist.

Application to the Court of Protection for the appointment or discharge of a trustee

Court of Protection Practice Direction 9F sets out the process for the following applications:

a) for the exercise of any power (including a power to consent) vested in P whether as a trustee or otherwise (section 18(1)(j) of the Mental Capacity Act 2005 (this includes section 39 Trustee Act 1925);

b) under section 36(9) of the Trustee Act 1925 for leave to appoint a new trustee in place of P;

c) under section 54 of the Trustee Act 1925 as to the court's jurisdiction;

d) under section 20 of the Trusts of Land and Appointment of Trustees Act 1996; or

e) for the court's approval of the appointment of a trustee in accordance with the terms of a trust.

Section 50(1) and paragraph 20(2) of Schedule 3 to the Mental Capacity Act 2005 and rule 8.2 of the Court of Protection Rules 2017 set out the circumstances in which permission of the Court of Protection to make an application is or is not required.

The application must be made using COP1 (and its relevant annexes, usually COP1D and COP12) and the following information must be provided as part of a COP24 (witness statement):

a) a copy of the existing trust document;

b) where relevant, a copy of any original conveyance, transfer, lease, assignment, settlement trust or will trust;

c) the names and addresses of any present trustees and details of any beneficial interest they have in the trust property. If the present trustees are not the original trustees, an explanation should be provided as to how they became trustees and copies of any deeds of appointment and retirement should be provided;

d) the full name, address and date of birth of any person proposed to replace P as a trustee, and details of that person's relationship to P;

e) confirmation that the trust is not under an order for administration in the Chancery Division;

f) if there is only one continuing trustee the applicant must confirm that both the trustee and the proposed new trustee have not made an enduring power of attorney or a lasting power of attorney in favour of the other party;

g) if an enduring power of attorney or a lasting power of attorney has been executed by a continuing trustee, a certified copy of that document must be provided. If the power has not been registered, the applicant must confirm that the trustee is still capable of carrying out his or her duties as a trustee;

h) the full name and address of any person who has an interest in any trust property as the beneficiary of a will, and whether any of them are children or persons who lack capacity;

i) if the proposed new trustee is not a solicitor or a trust corporation (for example, a bank) and has not been appointed as a deputy for the trustee lacking capacity, the applicant must provide a witness statement from a person independent of the application, wo has no interest in the trust property, attesting to the applicant's fitness to be appointed as trustee;

j) if the application relates to a transfer of assets in a will trust or similar settlement into the names of new trustees, accurate details of the trust assets must be provided (including full details of any stocks and shares held);

k) a copy of any notice of severance and evidence of service;

l) a copy of the will and grant of probate to the deceased's estate (where relevant);

m) confirmation of all relevant consents; and

n) a copy of a signed trustee's special undertaking.

Where the application relates to real property, the following additional information must be included:

a) the address of the property concerned, and whether it is freehold or leasehold;

b) the title number of the property and a copy of its entry in the Land Registry (if registered land). If the land is unregistered, the applicant should inform the court accordingly; and

c) if the property is leasehold the applicant should advise the court as to whether the applicant has a licence or consent to the assignment, and provide a copy of the same (or advise if a licence or consent is not necessary and the reason why it is not needed).

Incapacitated trustees: summary

P has capacity to retire as a trustee (and potentially appoint a replacement)	Will they consider retiring as a trustee? Usually this would be by way of deed.
The settlement makes provision for the removal of P as a trustee	Remove in accordance with the settlement. Note, a second trustee may need to be appointed.
The power of appointment or removal is vested in P	An application to the Court of Protection will be required pursuant to section 18(1)(j) MCA 2005
P needs to be removed as a trustee but no replacement necessary	An application to the Court of Protection will be required pursuant to section 39 Trustee Act 1925
Where P is a trustee with a beneficial interest and there are remaining trustees	An application to the Court of Protection will be required pursuant to section 36(9) Trustee Act 1925
Where P is a trustee without a beneficial interest and there are remaining trustees	P can be removed by deed pursuant to section 36(1) Trustee Act 1925
Where P is a trustee without a beneficial interest and there are no remaining trustees	An application to the High Court will be required pursuant to section 41 Trustee Act 1925 (but note no automatic vesting so an application to the Court of Protection pursuant to

	section 54 Trustee Act 1925 may be preferred)
Where P is a trustee without a beneficial interest and there are no remaining trustees	The beneficiaries (providing they are of full age, are capacitous and are absolutely entitled to the trust between them) can direct the appointment of a replacement trustee pursuant to section 20 Trusts of Land and Appointment of Trustees Act 1986
Where P is a trustee and no capable trustee and/or vesting required	An application to the Court of Protection pursuant to section 54 Trustee Act 1925 will be required but providing a deputy is appointed or an application for a deputy has been made
Where P has an attorney and has a beneficial interest in land	The attorney can exercise trustee functions pursuant to section 1(1) Trustee Delegation Act 1999 and can appoint an additional trustee if required (section 8 Trustee Delegation Act 1999)

Purchasing property on behalf of P

The attorney or deputy must be authorised to purchase property on behalf of P. There will usually be no limitations on an attorney's authority but a deputy is likely to require specific authority from the Court of Protection as the deputyship order will usually expressly exclude the power to purchase property.

Property purchased on behalf of P solely should be done so in P's name. Where the property is to be purchased jointly with another, the legal title will need to be vested in at least two trustees and a declaration of trust and Land Registry restriction (usually Form A) should be used to protect P's beneficial interest.

As noted above, a deputy cannot exercise trustee powers and as such, if the deputy is appointed as a property trustee they will be acting in that role and not as a deputy.

Acting as a director

The role of a director is a personal appointment. It cannot be delegated to an attorney or a deputy.

Where the director lacks capacity to act as a director, it will be necessary to consult the company's articles of association in order to ascertain whether there are any specific provisions with regard to the loss of mental capacity of a director. For companies incorporated after 28 April 2013, the model articles do not provide for automatic termination of a director's appointment upon a loss of capacity but will require a registered medical practitioner to provide a written opinion to the company stating that that person has become physically or mentally incapable of acting as a director and may remain so for more than three months (paragraph 18). For companies incorporated before this date, different provisions may apply.

Where the incapacitated director was the sole director, the articles may make provision as to how a replacement director is to be appointed. This power may ultimately lie with the shareholders.

Acting as a shareholder

An attorney or deputy will usually be authorised to exercise shareholder rights on behalf of an incapacitated shareholder, even if the appointment of director has been terminated. In this situation, the terms of the deputyship order or power of attorney should be consulted, together with the articles of association and any shareholder agreement.

Where the person who has lost capacity to act was a sole director and there are no contrary provision in the articles of association, as mentioned above the attorney or deputy may be able to exercise shareholder powers on behalf of the incapacitated person in order to appoint a new director or directors.

Managing financial affairs: appointment of a deputy

If the client lacks capacity to manage his or her affairs, it may be necessary for a third party to be authorised to manage the client's affairs on their behalf. The client may have already made provision for such circumstances by making an enduring power of attorney or lasting power of attorney. In the event no such provision has been made, or the provision is no longer relevant or applicable (for example if the attorney has died), it may be necessary for an application to be made to the Court of Protection for a deputy to be appointed.

An application for the appointment of a deputy must be made in accordance with part 9 of the Court of Protection Rules 2017 and by filing the following:

- application form (COP1) in duplicate;
- supporting information form (COP1A);
- assessment of capacity (COP3);
- deputy's declaration (COP4);
- application fee of £365 payable to HMCTS or through the HMCTS PBA system (note, a fee remission or exemption may be available)

On receipt of the application, the Court will issue the COP1 and return a copy of it to the applicant or their representative. At that point, P must be personally notified within 14 days of service of the issued application, using forms COP14 and COP5. Notice can be provided by the applicant or their representative. P must be told about the application and the purpose of it and if he or she wishes to object, he should complete (or be assisted to complete) form COP5 and return it to the Court.

Other interested persons, as identified in the application, must be notified in person, by first class post, by fax or by document exchange within 14 days of service of the application using forms COP15 and COP5. The Court usually requires three persons to be notified of the application and Court of Protection Practice Direction 9B sets out who these persons are. In the absence of family or friends, as set out in the Practice Direction, other persons to be notified include P's GP, social worker or care home manager.

Confirmation of service must be provided to the Court within 7 days of service being provided, using forms COP20A and COP20B. These should be filed together by email to COP_Service@judiciary.gov.uk.

Any objections to the application by P or other interested persons must be made within 14 days of service by filing a form COP5 and a form COP24. If someone wishes to object to the application who has not been formally notified of the application, they will need to submit a form COP1.

It is relatively unusual to include anyone as a respondent to the application. This is more relevant during ongoing contested proceedings.

The Court will notify the applicant that the order has been made but before copies of the order are released, the Court will usually require the deputy to obtain a security bond. This is a form of insurance policy and is used to protect P and his or her estate.

The Court will set the level of bond by reference to various factors and guidance about this can be found in the two judgments of *Baker v H* [2009] EWHC B31 (Fam) and *The Public Guardian v Matrix Deputies and the London Borough of Enfield and others* [2017] EWCOP 17, as well as in the Public Guardian's Guidance SD15 (which was published in 2015).

The bond premium is paid annually and the deputy should review the level of cover, making an application to the Court for reconsideration (both to increase and decrease the level of cover) if appropriate.

On receipt of the order, P must be notified in person for a second time, although it is usual for formal confirmation of notification to the court to be dispensed with.

It is necessary to check the terms of the order carefully, noting any restrictions on the authority of the deputy. One common restriction is regarding the disposal or acquisition of property on P's behalf. An application for reconsideration of the order should be made using form COP9 within 21 days of the Order being served.

The Public Guardian is responsible for the supervision of deputies. An initial deputy assessment fee of £100 is usually payable and ongoing supervision fees of £320 or £35 are paid annually from P's estate, depending on P's circumstances.

Deputies are required to submit an annual report to the Office of the Public Guardian using form OPG102, which can be completed online or print. This sets out details of the decisions made by the deputy during the previous year, as well as recording financial transactions.

Professional deputies are also required to estimate their fees for the next reporting period using form OPG105. Solicitors should continually review the estimate given in the OPG105 and in the event that they anticipate exceeding it by 20% or more, they should notify the Office of the Public Guardian accordingly. Failure to do so risks not being able to recover the additional costs.

Statutory will applications

If a client lacks capacity to make a will, it is necessary to consider whether an application to the Court of Protection for the execution of a statutory will on behalf of the client is needed. Examples of when a statutory will application may be appropriate include:

- Where a will has been incorrectly executed and P has lost capacity to re-execute.

- Where a legacy has adeemed, for example where a specific item has been disposed of during P's lifetime. Note, however, the saving provisions of section 18 and paragraph 8 of Schedule 2 of the MCA which states that where P's property, which is not just real property, is subject to a specific legacy in P's will and has been disposed of by a deputy, the legacy will not adeem and instead will apply to the property representing the property disposed of. If the property disposed of was real property, the property representing it is to be treated, so long as it remains part of P's estate, as if it were real property. Please note that this does not apply to disposals by attorneys or by P themselves. Furthermore, given the potential difficulties with identifying the proceeds of the disposed asset, it may be appropriate for a statutory will application to still be made.

- Other examples of when a statutory will may be appropriate, include:

    - Where there has been a major change in P's circumstances or in his relationship.

    - Where an executor or principal beneficiary has predeceased P and there are no adequate replacements.

    - Where there has been financial abuse.

    - Where P's existing will or his intestacy fails to make provision for people for whom, or purposes for which, P might be expected to provide and the result of not making a will would be unjust and contrary to P's best interests.

    - Where P has re-married since he made his last will.

This list is not exhaustive and an appropriate circumstance will be entirely case specific.

The court's principal powers in respect of P's property and affairs are contained in section 18 and Schedule 2 of the MCA. Section 18(1)(i) MCA gives the court authority specifically in relation to the execution of a will on behalf of a person who lacks capacity to make one for themselves. Authority must be granted expressly; a deputy or attorney has no automatic authority to execute a will on behalf of P.

A statutory will has the same effect for all purposes as if P had the capacity to make a valid will and the will had been executed by him in the manner required by the Wills Act 1837, except to the extent that it relates to:

- the disposal of immovable property outside England and Wales, or
- insofar as it relates to any other property or matter if, when the will is executed:
    - P is domiciled outside England and Wales; and
    - under the law of P's domicile, any questions of his testamentary capacity would fall to be determined in accordance with the law of a place outside England and Wales

in those circumstances, the practitioner should seek advice from a lawyer in that jurisdiction.

All decisions made on behalf of or in respect of a person who lacks capacity, including in relation to statutory wills, must be made pursuant to the principles of the MCA as set out in section 1. In particular, the court will only authorise a statutory will if it is in P's best interests to do so. It will try to avoid becoming involved in family disputes but in *Re D (VAC v FKD)* [2010] EWHC 2159, for example, it was considered that it would not be in P's best interests for her to be remembered for having left a contentious Probate dispute to her family.

The court has also applied the "right thing" test in a number of cases, including in *Re P* [2009] EWHC 163 (Ch) where Mr Justice Lewison stated: "For many people it is in their best interests that they be remembered with affection by their family as having done the right thing by their will" and in Re M where Mr Justice Munby noted "We have an interest in being remembered as having done the "right thing", either in life, or, post-mortem, by will."

This is likely to be of less relevance where there already exists evidence of P's past and present wishes, feelings, beliefs and values, particularly where they run counter to doing the "right thing', for example in *Re JC* [2012] COPLR 540 where Senior Judge Lush noted "JC has an appalling track record. He has spent his entire lifetime doing precisely "the wrong thing" in his relationship with others…".

The cases of *Re G (TJ)* [2010] EWHC 3005 (COP) and *Re M* [2009] EWHC 2525 both consider at length the issue of best interests. In Re G(TJ) Mr Justice Morgan determined that best interests involves a number of factors, including:

- the actual wishes of P
- the beliefs and values which would be likely to influence P's decision
- other factors which P would be likely to consider if he had capacity to do so
- balance sheet of factors which P would draw up if he had capacity to do so

Although Mr Justice Morgan accepted that there will be an element of substituted judgment, he emphasised that it is absolutely clear that the ultimate test for the court is the test of best interests and not the test of substituted judgment.

It can be particularly difficult to ascertain P's best interests where P has never been able to express any relevant testamentary wishes or form any obvious beliefs and values. In *Re D (J)* [1982] Ch 237, although a pre-MCA case, Hoffman noted: "I recognise the difficulty in forming a view of what might have been expected from a person who has never enjoyed a rational; mind. But I think that in those circumstances the court must assume that she would have been a normal decent person, acting in accordance with contemporary standards of morality. In the absence of actual evidence to the contrary, no less should be assumed of any person and in this case there is nothing to displace such an assumption".

As such, there is likely to be an element of substituted judgment and given the speculative nature of establishing what factors P would be likely to consider in these types of cases, it will often be necessary to show why the intestacy provisions would be inappropriate.

Extending the consideration of best interests, Mr Justice Munby in *Re M* stated:

- There is no hierarchy between the various factors in section 4, that is, the best interests section of the MCA, beyond the overarching principle that what is determinative is the judicial evaluation of what is in P's best interests.

- The weight to be attached to the various section 4 factors will differ depending upon the individual circumstances of the particular case. A feature or factor which in one case may carry great, possibly even preponderant, weight may in another, superficially similar, case carry much less, or even very little, weight.

- There may be one or more features or factors which are of magnetic importance in influencing or even determining the outcome.

- P's wishes and feelings will be a significant factor to which the court must pay close regard. The weight to be attached to those wishes and feelings will always be case specific and fact specific and in considering the weight and importance to be attached to P's wishes and feelings the court must have regard to all the relevant circumstances. These circumstances include:

    1. The degree of P's incapacity.

    2. The strength and consistency of the views expressed by P.

3. The possible impact on P of knowing that his wishes and feelings have not been given effect to.

4. The extent to which P's wishes and feelings are, or are not, rational, sensible, responsible and pragmatically capable of implementation.

5. The extent to which P's wishes and feelings, if given effect, can properly be accommodated within the court's overall assessment of what is in his best interests.

Mr Justice Munby also reiterated that best interests do not cease at the moment of death and this may extend to avoiding post-death litigation.

The procedure for making an application for a statutory will can be found in Part 9 of the Court of Protection Rules 2017 and Practice Direction 9(e). The forms to be filed are:

- COP1 (application form).

- COP1A (supporting information for property and financial affairs) although this is not always required as the information is usually covered by the COP24 (witness statement). If there is any doubt, the COP1A should be included.

- COP1C (supporting information for statutory will applications)

- COP3 assessment of capacity. This must specifically address the capacity to make a will. The form focuses on the MCA test of capacity it must specifically address the *Banks v Goodfellow* test.

- COP24 witness statement containing the supporting documentation set out in Practice Direction 9(e) which includes:

    - the draft will

    - any existing will

    - any consents to act by proposed executors

  - the family tree
  - a schedule of P's assets with up-to-date valuations
  - an up-to-date report of P's present medical condition, life expectancy and testamentary capacity

- The court fee, currently £365

Section 50(1) and paragraph 20(2) of Schedule 3 to the MCA and Rule 8.2 of the Court of Protection Rules 2017 set out the circumstances in which permission is, or is not, required to make an application for a statutory will.

Certain categories of Applicant do not require permission to apply and this includes:

- P's deputy
- The Public Guardian
- The Official Solicitor
- A donee of a Lasting Power of Attorney

The COP24 is the key part of the application and should include the information set out in Practice Direction 9(e):

(a) copy of the draft will or codicil, plus one copy;

(b) a copy of any existing will or codicil;

(c) any consents to act by proposed executors;

(d) details of P's family, preferably in the form of a family tree, including details of the full name and date of birth of each person included in the family tree. The assistance of a genealogist may be required;

(e) a schedule showing details of P's current assets, with up to date valuations;

(f) a schedule showing the estimated net yearly income and spending of P;

(g) a statement showing P's needs, both current and future estimates, and P's general circumstances;

(h) if P is living in National Health Service accommodation, information on whether P may be discharged to local authority accommodation, to other fee-paying accommodation or to P's own home;

(i) if the applicant considers it relevant, full details of the resources of any proposed beneficiary, and details of any likely changes if the application is successful;

(j) details of any capital gains tax, inheritance tax or income tax which may be chargeable in respect of the subject matter of the application;

(k) an explanation of the effect, if any, that the proposed changes will have on P's circumstances, preferably in the form of a 'before and after' schedule of assets and income;

(l) if appropriate, a statement of whether any land would be affected by the proposed will or settlement and if so, details of its location and title number, if applicable;

(m) where the application is for a settlement of property or for the variation of an existing settlement or trust, a draft of the proposed deed, plus one copy;

(n) a copy of any registered enduring power of attorney or lasting power of attorney. I would add to this a copy of any deputyship order;

(o) confirmation that P is a resident of England or Wales; and

(p) an up to date report of P's present medical condition, life expectancy, likelihood of requiring increased expenditure in the foreseeable future, and testamentary capacity.

The practitioner must also ensure:

- the COP24 addresses why the applicant is seeking the statutory will. There needs to be a good reason to depart from the terms of the current will or intestacy provisions;
- it is explained why P's circumstances have changed; and
- it is explained why the statutory will is in P's best interests. When considering best interests, the practitioner should address each element of section 4 individually, remembering there is no hierarchy or individual element of magnetic importance. Consider P's wishes and feelings by meeting with him and if the practitioner's firm has acted for P previously, consider if there is anything in the old files which indicates his past wishes and feelings, although remembering the duty of confidentiality to the client.

If the practitioner does not feel comfortable drafting the COP24, counsel can be instructed to assist with this, or with any part of the application, and the costs of this will usually be paid from P's funds.

Practice Direction 9(e) sets out the respondents and persons who must be notified of an application. The applicant must name as a respondent:

- any beneficiary under an existing will or codicil who is likely to be materially or adversely affected by the application;
- any beneficiary under a proposed will or codicil who is likely to be materially or adversely affected by the application; and
- any respective beneficiary under P's intestacy where P has no existing, or valid, will.

When considering who may fall into the categories to be served, regard should be had as to P's life expectancy, and who might foreseeably be affected by the terms of the application if P were to not die imminently.

If any of the respondents are under the age of 18, or lack capacity to conduct the proceedings, they will require a litigation friend.

A litigation friend is a person who can fairly and competently conduct proceedings on behalf of a child or a protected party (that is, a person who by reason of mental disorder is incapable of managing and administering his own affairs).

In Court of Protection proceedings, the court will consider at the earliest opportunity whether P should be joined as a party to the proceedings, and, if P is so joined, the court will consider whether the Official Solicitor should be invited to act as litigation friend, or whether some other person should be appointed to act in that role.

Rule 17.1 of the Court of Protection Rules provides that a person may act as a litigation friend on behalf of a person who lacks capacity if that person:

- can fairly and competently conduct proceedings on behalf of that person; and
- has no interests adverse to those of that person.

Usual practice is for the Official Solicitor to act as litigation friend. In *Re D* it was stated the reasons for this are:

- he can conduct the proceedings fairly and competently;
- he has no interests adverse to P's interests;
- he has considerable experience and expertise in relation to the discharge of his role as litigation friend in cases of this kind; and
- as the Official Solicitor to the Senior Court, he has a broader remit as advocate to those courts, to provide them with advice

and assistance, including guidance on the impact of any decision a Judge may make.

The role of the litigation friend is considered further below.

Once the application has been issued, the court will usually make an initial directions order:

- to join P as a party
- to invite the Official Solicitor to act as litigation friend
- to direct the respondents to be served and any other persons to be notified. Respondents need to be served a full copy of the application; persons to be notified only need to be notified using form COP15.
- to direct the respondents to respond by way of COP5 and potentially COP24
- to direct the parties to report back to the court within 12 weeks to confirm whether agreement is likely, further time is required or whether the matter needs to be listed for a hearing

The requirement to serve those affected by a statutory will has been judicially described at representing "a principle of natural justice, which deters a judge from making a decision that impacts adversely on the rights of an individual without giving him the opportunity to be heard".

Rules 6.10 and 7.11 of the Court of Protection Rules 2017 permit the court to dispense with service of others and of P.

The decision to dispense with service is not a decision made by reference to P's best interests, instead "[the] decision is one made by one judge in exercise of powers given by the Court of Protection Rules. It is not an act done or a decision made on behalf of P. The principles of the Mental Capacity Act 2005 cannot be strictly applied to such a decision".

Dispensing with service will be permitted only in exceptional circumstances where there are compelling reasons for doing so. Examples of circumstances where full service may not be required include:

1. if there is only a modest departure from the status quo being proposed
2. if the applicant has taken all reasonable steps to trace the current intestate successors without success
3. the conduct of the respondent may exceptionally justify service being dispensed with, for example if the respondent had been convicted of physical or sexual abuse of P or where P's funds derive from a CICA award where P was the assailant.

Agreement to not serve P is even less likely to be agreed. The example shown on the screen does not relate to a statutory will application and extends only as to whether full disclosure of a PI settlement should be given to P.

The practitioner should assume that permission will not be granted and an application to dispense with service should be made only in exceptional circumstances.

Rule 9.12 relates to objections made by a party or someone notified of an application. If a person who has been served as a notified person or as a Respondent to the proceedings wishes to object, they should file a COP5 within 14 days of service and a COP24 within 28 days of service.

For those who are not a party to the proceedings, they can apply pursuant to Rule 9.15 of the Court of Protection Rules to be joined and this is done by filing a form COP9 and a form COP24. The COP24 should include evidence of that person's interest in the proceedings and, if that person proposes that an order different from that set out in the application form should be made, the evidence on which that person intends to rely.

The court must consider whether to join the person applying under this rule as a party to the proceedings and, if it decides to do so, it must make an order to that effect.

The parties should seek to reach agreement as amicably as possible, at the least cost to P's estate. The court may direct mediation or a dispute resolution hearing but the parties should be proactively considering this in any case. It can be useful to narrow the issues of dispute before any mediation, so as to achieve the most from the time available at the mediation (or dispute resolution hearing).

Once the order has been made, the will needs to be signed. The execution requirements are set out in paragraph 3(2) of Schedule 2 to the MCA. Those are:

- the will must state that it is signed by P acting by the authorised person;
- the will must be signed by the authorised person with the name of P and his own name, in the presence of two or more witnesses present at the same time;
- the will must be attested and subscribed by those witnesses in the presence of the authorised person; and
- it must be sealed with the official seal of the court.

Once the will has been signed, the original and two copies must be sent to the court for sealing. The court seals the original and one copy and returns both to the applicant. The applicant's solicitor is usually required to sign an undertaking to hold the will in safe custody for P's life.

If P dies before the will has been sealed, the will is still valid. *Re Hughes* ChD 8 Jan 1999 confirms that sealing is an administrative act only.

It is likely to take several months for the application to be completed, although the court does have a procedure for dealing with urgent matters. Remember that what the practitioner considers urgent may not be shared by the court and this procedure should not be used as a matter of course.

Common reasons for delay include:

1. not including all the exhibits and information required by Practice Direction 9(E) and updating it during proceedings where appropriate;

2. COP3 not addressing testamentary capacity specifically;

3. not properly identifying respondents ;

4. where P has limited cash funds, as the Official Solicitor may be unwilling to act and it can be difficult to locate another suitable litigation friend.

Conducting litigation

If P lacks capacity to conduct litigation, there are two options:

1. for someone to be authorised by the Court of Protection to conduct litigation in the name of an on behalf of P;

2. for someone to be appointed as litigation friend

No third party has an automatic right to conduct litigation on behalf of an incapacitated person.

<u>Litigation for and on behalf of the incapacitated client</u>

A deputy (or attorney) does not have authority to conduct litigation. Where such authority is required, an application should be made to the Court of Protection for it to exercise its powers pursuant to section 16 MCA and more specifically, section 18(1)(k) MCA (the conduct of legal proceedings in P's name or on P's behalf).

In *ACC & Ors (property and affairs deputy; recovering assets costs for legal proceedings)* [2020] EWCOP 9 (27 February 2020), the Court of Protection determined that the line between a deputy seeking advice and conducting litigation stops short of formal issue of proceedings. A deputy must be careful not act outside the terms of their authority and may be at personal risk as to costs if they do so. This also applies to attorneys.

When the court considers the application for authority to conduct litigation on behalf of P, it will need to consider some evidence of the prospects of success of the proposed litigation. It will also consider whether there should be limits to such authority. If there are concerns as to merits or costs or otherwise, the authority may be (and often is) granted only up to a specified stage of proceedings (when another merits assessment may be required), or with a limit on the costs which may be incurred without further application. The court will sometimes also do this when it is granting authority to a deputy to carry out preliminary investigations as to whether litigation should be pursued.

Where a deputy or attorney has acted without authority and subsequently seeks retrospective authorisation from the Court of Protection, they must be aware of *Re Nottley* (1839) 3 Jur (OS) 719 where it was stated "it would be very singular, indeed, that a party could find time to get up actions, and yet could not, as he alleged, find time to apply to the court for its sanction … the petition must be refused with costs". The Senior Judge in *ACC* did not suggest that the robust approach of *Re Nottley* will always be appropriate "but there is a force in the observation that if a deputy has been able to take the urgent action, they should also be able to make the application for a retrospective authorisation hard upon its heels". In the situation of an urgent injunction being sought on P's behalf, the deputy should clearly indicate their exposure and seek urgent consideration by the court. The deputy will also need to explain why a matter was so urgent that authority could not be sought prospectively.

The Senior Judge made it clear that the court cannot give any general or prospective assurance of the outcome of any application for retrospective approval; the court's determination of applications must be made in the best interests of P.

In summary, make the application as promptly as possible and ideally before the authority is required.

The effect of the Court of Protection authorising a deputy to conduct proceedings on behalf of P is:

(a) it gives the deputy priority over others in the hierarchy of potential litigation friends for P; and

(b) it enables the deputy to use P's funds to meet the reasonable costs of the litigation and to pay a costs order made against him in the proceedings (and as such, it is usually preferable for a deputy to be granted express authority to conduct litigation by the Court of Protection, rather than being appointed as litigation friend by the court seized of the proceedings).

Litigation friend

CPR 21 and the associated Practice Direction deal with children and protected parties. A protected party is a party, or an intended party, who "lacks capacity to conduct proceedings". Capacity is determined using the test set out in the Mental Capacity Act 2005 ("MCA 2005").

CPR 21.2(1) provides that a protected party must have a litigation friend to conduct proceedings on his behalf.

CPR 21.4 deals with who may be a litigation friend without a court order. CPR 21.4(3) provides that a person may act as a litigation friend if he:

> "(a) can fairly and competently conduct proceedings on behalf of the child or protected party;
>
> (b) has no interest adverse to that of the child or protected party; and
>
> (c) where the child or protected party is a claimant, undertakes to pay any costs which the child or protected party may be ordered to pay in relation to the proceedings, subject to any right he may have to be repaid from the assets of the child or protected party".

Where no deputy has been appointed by the Court of Protection with authority to conduct proceedings, the procedure is governed by CPR 21.5(3) which provides that (where the protected person is the claimant) the person must file a certificate of suitability at the time the claim is made.

CPR 21.6 provides that the court may make an order appointing a litigation friend. An application may be made either by the person who wishes to be the litigation friend or by a party, and must be supported by evidence. The two preconditions to the exercise of the court's power under CPR 21.6 are, first whether a party is a protected party and secondly, whether the requirements of CPR 21.4(3) (set out above) are met.

In relation to capacity, Mrs Justice Falk stated that there are two elements to section 2(1) MCA 2005, namely (a) an inability to make a decision in relation to the matter and (b) that the inability is the result of an impairment or disturbance of the kind described. Section 3 MCA 2005 provides that a person is unable to make a decision for himself if he unable to understand the information relevant to that decision, retain it, use it or weigh it as part of the process of making the decision, or communicate it. As set out in *Masterman-Lister v Brutton* [2003] 1 WLR 1511 (the leading case law on capacity to conduct litigation), "the key question is whether the party is capable of understanding, with the assistance of proper explanation from legal advisers and other experts as the case may require, the issues on which his consent or decision is likely to be necessary: does he have the "capacity to understand that which he needs to understand in order to pursue or defend a claim"?".

In an article by Alex Ruck Keene, Peter Bartlett and Neil Allen, the wider issue of the role of a litigation friend is considered, particularly whether 1) a litigation friend is under a duty to act in MCA best interests (which is Mrs Justice Falk's understanding of their role – see paragraphs 67 and 75 in particular) and 2) whether (even if they are) that requires them to act as gate-keeper to determine what arguments to advance on behalf of P are. The full note can be found at https://academic.oup.com/medlaw/article/24/3/333/2733263?keytype=ref&ijkey=gsPTUKu0OSlcdfY.

Persons seeking to be appointed as litigation friend should usually seek authorisation of the Court of Protection to conduct proceedings for P and on P's behalf. The key benefit of doing so is that that it offers protection for the litigation friend against costs orders and authorises P's funds to be used to pay the costs of litigation. It is possible for retrospective authority to be obtained, although the Court of Protection may query why there is a delay in making the application. Senior Judge Hilder's judgment in *ACC & Ors* considers litigation on behalf of P in more detail.

Acting on behalf of P in relation to divorce and associated financial proceedings

Section 27 MCA prohibits anyone (attorney, deputy, the court or otherwise) from consenting to a decree of divorce being granted on the basis of two years' separation (section 27(1)(c) MCA) or consenting to a dissolution order being made in relation to a civil partnership on the basis of two years' separation. In other situations, and attorney or deputy may have authority but it will usually be appropriate for express authority of the Court of Protection to be sought.

As mentioned above, attorneys and deputies do not have authority to conduct litigation on behalf of an incapacitated person and would either need to obtain express authority from the Court of Protection to conduct litigation (authority to consent to the divorce could also be obtained as part of the same application) or for them to be appointed as litigation friend by the court seized of the proceedings. For the reasons set out above, the preferable route would be to obtain express litigation authority from the Court of Protection.

Acting as personal representative

A person entitled to act as a personal representative under Rules 20 or 22 Non-Contentious Probate Rules 1987 cannot act in that capacity if he or she lacks capacity (pursuant to the Mental Capacity Act 2005) to do so. In that situation, Rule 35 of the NCPR 1987 sets out the order of priority as to who can act.

"Where a registrar is satisfied that a person entitled to a grant is by reason of mental incapacity incapable of managing his affairs, administration for his use and benefit, limited until further representation be granted or in such other way as the registrar may direct, may be granted in the following order of priority—

(a) to the person authorised by the Court of Protection to apply for a grant;

(b) where there is no person so authorised, to the lawful attorney of the incapable person acting under a registered enduring power of attorney;

(c) where there is no such attorney entitled to act, or if the attorney shall renounce administration for the use and benefit of the incapable person, to the person entitled to the residuary estate of the deceased."

Person authorised by the Court of Protection

Specific authority to apply for a grant on behalf of an incapacitated personal representative must be obtained from the Court of Protection – a standard deputyship order is insufficient – and the order will need to be produced with the application for the grant.

Notice to the Court of Protection

Where a person lacks capacity to act as a personal representative and no specific authorisation has been given to another to apply for the grant, notice must be given to the Court of Protection of the intended application for a discretionary grant.

Medical certificate

Where an application is being made pursuant to Rule 35(2)(c) NCPR, a medical certificate confirming incapacity will usually be required in the following form:

[name of practitioner and/or institution]

[name of patient]

I certify that:

The above-named patient [who is now residing in this institution] suffers from an impairment of, or a disturbance in the functioning of, the mind or brain as a result of which he is unable to make a decision for himself in relation to making an application for a grant representation and administration of the estate of [name] and in my opinion he lacks capacity to manage his property and affairs within the meaning of the Mental Capacity Act 2005.

Date:

(signed)

[name]

Alternatively, a form of medical certificate (PA14) can be used. This can be downloaded from www.gov.uk/government/publications/form-pa14-medical-certificate-probate.

CHAPTER SEVENTEEN

COSTS AND FEES IN THE COURT OF PROTECTION

Court of Protection fees

As at 1 April 2020, the fees charged by the Court are set out in the Schedule to the Court of Protection Fees Order 2007 (SI 2007/1745) (as amended by the Court of Protection Fees (Amendment) Order 2019 (SI 2019/1063)):

- Application fee – £365: payable on making an application to start court proceedings or on making an application for permission to start proceedings.

- Appeal fee – £230: payable on filing an appellants notice appealing a court decision or seeking permission to appeal a court decision.

- Hearing fee – £485: payable where the court has held a hearing to decide the application and has made a final order, declaration or decision.

- Copy of document fee – £5: payable on requesting a copy of a document filed during court proceedings.

An application fee is payable on the making of any application under Part 9 of the Court of Protection Rules 2017. This applies to all applications, whether made by deputies, attorneys, donees or other persons. An application fee is also payable on an application for permission although, if permission is given, it is not payable again on the making of the application.

No fee is payable on the following applications:

- where an application is made within the proceedings on an application notice (Part 10 of the CoPR 2017 procedure);

- on a first application where an application for permission has been made and permission has been granted (art 4(2));
- where a person who has been served with or notified of an application and wishes to take part in proceedings (under rule 9.12 of the CoPR 2017);
- where an application is made under rule 9.7 of the CoPR 2017 by the donee or a person named in a lasting power of attorney (LPA) and the application is solely in respect of an objection to the registration of the LPA;
- where an application is made under rule 9.7 of the Court of Protection Rules 2017 by the donee or a person named in a lasting power of attorney (LPA) and the application is solely in respect of an objection to the registration of the LPA;
- where an application is made under rule 9.8 of the CoPR 2017 by a donor, attorney or notified person and the application is solely in respect of an objection to the registration of an enduring power of attorney (EPA);
- where the application is made by the Public Guardian; and
- where P dies within five days of an application being made (art 4(5)).

Furthermore, it was announced on 1 December that court fees in relation to applications made for access to Child Trust Funds may be waived in some circumstances. See https://www.gov.uk/government/news/child-trust-fund-court-fees-waived-for-parents for more information.

Exemption and remission

If P is entitled to a 'qualifying benefit' (except where P is also entitled to a personal injury award) then the fee payable is remitted in full. The Court of Protection remission policy is also extended to cases where P is not in receipt of a 'qualifying benefit' but has a gross income below £16,500. Depending on the level of P's income, fees may be remitted in whole or in part as follows:

Income	*Percentage of fee remitted*
Up to £12,000	No fee payable
£12,001 to £13,500	75% remission
£13,501 to £15,000	50% remission
£15,001 to £16,500	25% remission
Over £16,500	No remission – the full fee is payable

The Court may also exercise its discretion within the scope of article 9 to remit fees where payment may cause P undue hardship.

Further details and the remission application form (form COP44A) can be found at www.gov.uk/government/publications/apply-for-help-with-court-of-protection-fees-form-cop44a.

Solicitors' costs

Costs in proceedings – the general rule

Costs incurred in any proceedings are governed by Part 19 of the Court of Protection Rules 2017 in addition to Parts 44, 47 and 48 of the Civil Procedure Rules. Rule 19.2 sets out the following general rule in relation to property and affairs applications:

"Where the proceedings concern P's property and affairs the general rule is that the costs of the proceedings or of that part of the proceedings that concerns P's property and affairs, shall be paid by P or charged to his estate".

Rule 19.3 deals with personal welfare applications and the general rule is that there will be no order as to the costs of the proceedings or of that part of the proceedings that concerns P's personal welfare.

Rule 19.5 allows the court to depart from the general rule 'if the circumstances so justify'. The court must have regard to all the circumstances, including the conduct of the parties, whether a party has succeeded on part of his case, even if he has not been wholly successful; and the role of any public body involved in the proceedings. Rule 19.5(2) defines conduct of the parties as including:

(a) conduct before, as well as during, the proceedings;

(b) whether it was reasonable for a party to raise, pursue or contest a particular issue;

(c) the manner in which a party has made or responded to an application or a particular issue; and

(d) whether a party who has succeeded in his application or response to an application, in whole or in part, exaggerated any matter contained in his application or response.

The standard provision for costs in relation to deputyship applications and ongoing costs is as follows:

"The deputy is entitled to receive fixed costs in relation to this application, and to receive costs for the general management of [P]'s affairs [at the public authority/solicitors' rate]. If the deputy would prefer the costs to be assessed, this order is to be treated as authority to the Senior Court's Costs Office to carry out a detailed assessment on the standard basis".

<u>Solicitors' fixed costs</u>

Court of Protection Practice Direction 19B deals with costs. Fixed costs are set out as follow:

Category	*Type of work*	*Fee (plus VAT)*
Category I	Work up to and including the date upon which the court makes an order appointing a deputy for property and affairs.	£900

Category	*Type of work*	*Fee (plus VAT)*
Category II	Applications under s 36(9) or s 54 Trustee Act 1925 or s 20 Trusts of Land and Appointment of Trustees Act 1996 for the appointment of a new trustee in the place of P and applications under s 18(1)(j) MCA 2005 for authority to exercise any power vested in P, whether beneficially, or as trustee, or otherwise.	£500
Category III (where a solicitor acts as a deputy)	Annual management fee where the court appoints a professional deputy for property and affairs, payable on the anniversary of the court order.	a. For the first year: £1,670 b. For the second and subsequent years: £1,320 Provided that, where the net assets of P are below £16,000, the professional deputy for property and affairs may take an annual management fee not exceeding 4.5% of P's net assets on the anniversary of the court order appointing the professional as deputy
Category IV	Where the court appoints a professional deputy for health and welfare.	The deputy may take an annual management fee not exceeding 2.5% of P's net assets on the anniversary of the court order appointing the professional as deputy

Category	*Type of work*	*Fee (plus VAT)*
		for health and welfare up to a maximum of £550
Category V	Preparation and lodgement of the annual report or annual account to the Public Guardian.	£265
Category VI	a) Preparation of a basic HMRC income tax return (bank or NS&I interest and taxable benefits, discretionary trust or estate income) on behalf of P.	An amount not exceeding £250 (plus VAT)
	b) Preparation of a complex HMRC income tax return (bank or NS&I interest, multiple investment portfolios, taxable benefits, one or more rental properties) on behalf of P.	An amount not exceeding £600 (plus VAT)

Detailed assessment

Rule 19.6 of the Court of Protection Rules 2017, Parts 43, 44, 47 and 48 of the Civil Procedure Rules govern the assessment of solicitors' costs which is the usual way of determining the proper costs payable to a solicitor in legal proceedings. If a party is permitted costs, the order determining the application or a separate order dealing with costs will provide for costs to be assessed if fixed costs or agreed costs are not applicable. Costs are usually awarded on the standard basis and are payable from P's estate.

Where costs are payable pursuant to an order of the court, then the amount that can be charged is in accordance with the court's guidelines set out in the Guide to the Summary Assessment of Costs published by the Senior Courts Costs Office and the Guideline Hourly Rates as follows:

Categories of fee earner

(A) Solicitors with over eight years' post qualification experience including at least eight years' litigation experience.

(B) Solicitors and legal executives with over four years' post qualification experience including at least four years' litigation experience.

(C) Other solicitors and legal executives and fee earners of equivalent experience.

(D) Trainee solicitors, paralegals and other fee earners.

Rates

Since 1 April 2010 the rates (showing the relevant localities) are as shown in the document online at https://www.gov.uk/guidance/solicitors-guideline-hourly-rates

Band	*Rate*	*Locality*
National One	A £217 B £192 C £161 D £118	Aldershot, Farnham, Bournemouth (including Poole), Birmingham Inner, Bristol, Cambridge City, Harlow, Canterbury, Maidstone, Medway & Tunbridge Wells, Cardiff (Inner), Chelmsford South, Essex & East Suffolk, Chester, Fareham, Winchester, Hampshire, Dorset, Wiltshire, Isle of Wight, Kingston, Guildford, Reigate, Epsom, Leeds Inner (within a 2km radius of the City Art Gallery), Lewes, Liverpool, Birkenhead, Manchester Central, Newcastle – City Centre (within a two-mile radius of St Nicholas

		Cathedral), Norwich City, Nottingham City, Oxford, Thames Valley, Southampton, Portsmouth, Swindon, Basingstoke, Watford
National Two	A £201 B £177 C £146 D £111	Bath, Cheltenham and Gloucester, Taunton, Yeovil, Bury, Chelmsford North, Cambridge County, Peterborough, Bury St E, Norfolk, Lowestoft, Cheshire & North Wales, Coventry, Rugby, Nuneaton, Stratford and Warwick, Exeter, Plymouth, Hull (City), Leeds Outer, Wakefield & Pontefract, Leigh, Lincoln, Luton, Bedford, St Albans, Hitchin, Hertford, Manchester Outer, Oldham, Bolton, Tameside, Newcastle (other than City Centre), Nottingham & Derbyshire, Sheffield, Doncaster and South Yorkshire, Southport, St Helens, Stockport, Altrincham, Salford, Swansea, Newport, Cardiff (Outer), Wigan, Wolverhampton, Walsall, Dudley & Stourbridge, York, Harrogate
National Three	A £201 B £177 C £146 D £111	Birmingham Outer, Bradford (Dewsbury, Halifax, Huddersfield, Keighley & Skipton), Cumbria, Devon, Cornwall, Grimsby, Skegness, Hull Outer, Kidderminster, Northampton & Leicester, Preston, Lancaster, Blackpool, Chorley, Accrington, Burnley, Blackburn, Rawtenstall & Nelson, Scarborough & Ripon, Stafford, Stoke, Tamworth, Teesside, Worcester, Hereford, Evesham, and Redditch, Shrewsbury, Telford, Ludlow, Oswestry, South & West Wales

London	A £409 B £296 C £226 D £138	City of London: EC1, EC2, EC3, EC4
London	A £317 B £242 C £196 D £126	Central London: W1, WC1, WC2, SW1
London	A £229–267 B £172–229 C £165 D £121	Outer London: (All other London post codes: W, NW, N, E, SE, SW and Bromley, Croydon, Dartford, Gravesend and Uxbridge)

Following Master Whalan's decision in *Re PLK, Thakur, Chapman & Tate* (SCCO Refs: 13080340, 12177963, 11775290 and 11620036), costs officers assessing Court of Protection matters have been given some flexibility when applying the guideline hourly rates. Following the judgment, where the hourly rates claimed fall within 120% of the guideline hourly rates, Master Whalan determined that these should be considered as reasonable. These "PLK rates" are as follows:

Bands	A	B	C	D
London 1	£490	£355	£271	£165
London 2	£380	£290	£235	£151
London 3	£275–320	£206–275	£198	£145
National 1	£260	£230	£193	£142
National 2	£241	£212	£175	£133

APPENDICES

APPENDIX 1

RESOURCES

- Mental Capacity Act 2005
    - https://www.legislation.gov.uk/ukpga/2005/9/contents
- Mental Capacity Act 2005 Code of Practice
    - https://www.gov.uk/government/publications/mental-capacity-act-code-of-practice
- Court of Protection Rules 2017
    - https://www.legislation.gov.uk/uksi/2017/1035/contents/made
- Court of Protection Practice Directions
    - https://www.judiciary.uk/publications/court-of-protection-practice-directions/
- Office of the Public Guardian Guidance Notes
    - https://www.gov.uk/government/organisations/office-of-the-public-guardian
- Law Society Practice Note: Meeting the needs of vulnerable clients
    - https://www.lawsociety.org.uk/support-services/advice/practice-notes/meeting-the-needs-of-vulnerable-clients-july-2015/
- Everyday Decision Research Project

    - www.legalcapacity.org.uk/everyday-decisions/supported-will-making-report

- HM Land Registry Practice Guide 9: powers of attorney and registered land

    - https://www.gov.uk/government/publications/powers-of-attorney-and-registered-land/practice-guide-9-powers-of-attorney-and-registered-land

APPENDIX 2

PRECEDENT ATTENDANCE NOTE (ASSESSMENT OF CAPACITY ELEMENT ONLY)

Client name	
Client reference	
Date of meeting	
Format of meeting (in person/video etc)	
Question to be considered	
The legal test	
The relevant law	

Questions asked	
Answers received	
How the test of capacity was satisfied	
Next steps	
Substantive record of attendance	

APPENDIX 3

LETTER OF INSTRUCTION TO AN INDEPENDENT ASSESSOR

LTR Blank Letter to Adhoc capacity (MMGR0001)

Dear Dr X

NAME OF CLIENT

DATE OF BIRTH

ADDRESS

I have been instructed by [client] to [prepare a [will] [lasting power of attorney in respect of [property and financial affairs] [and] [or] [health and welfare]]] [advise in relation to a gift].

[I am aware that [client] has been diagnosed with [dementia of mixed Alzheimer's/Vascular type]. Given this diagnosis and the nature of the instructions I have received, I should be grateful if you would carry out an assessment into [client]'s capacity to make the [will] [lasting power[s] of attorney] [gift].

The general test of capacity for our purposes is set out in the Mental Capacity Act 2005. This states that a person lacks capacity in relation to a matter if, on the balance of probabilities, the individual has an impairment of or a disturbance in the functioning of the mind or brain and the effect of this is that the individual is unable to make the specific decision at the time the decision needs to be made. A person is unable to make the decision for herself in relation to a given matter if, with appropriate assistance if necessary, the person is unable to understand the information relevant to the decision, to retain that information, to use or weigh that information as part of the process of making the decision or to communicate their decision by whatever means. A person should not be treated as unable to make a decision even if the relevant information can only be retained for a short period of time.

The Mental Capacity Act 2005 also provides that a person should not be treated as unable to make a decision unless all practicable steps to help them to do so have been taken without success, such as explaining or presenting the information in different ways, choosing a location where the person feels more at ease, choosing a time of day when the person's understanding is better, obtaining the help of a family member or postponing the decision if the disturbance or impairment is temporary. [Therefore, if you consider [client]'s capacity may fluctuate, please let me know if we should arrange our meeting for another time or date.]

I have set out the specific tests of capacity with regard to the decisions we are concerned with below.

<u>Will</u>

You need only show on the balance of probability whether [client] has or does not have a testamentary capacity, in other words, that it is more likely than not. Please would you consider the following points in particular, and indicate whether [client] understands them:

1. The nature of the act of making a will. This involves understanding that [s]he will die and that when she does the will comes into operation. Further, [s]he can change or revoke the will before [her][his] death but only for as long as [s]he has the mental capacity to do so.

2. The effect of making a will. This includes the appointment of executors, deciding who receives what, whether the gifts are outright, consequences of a depleted estate, that a beneficiary may predecease [her] [him], and the effect on any previous will.

3. The extent of the estate. This includes the amount of property or money or investments [s]he holds and the fact that some may be jointly owned, that some benefits may be

payable only on [her] [his] death irrespective of [her] [his] will and that the estate may change during [her] [his] lifetime.

4. The possible claims of others. Beneficiaries may be left out because of other adequate provision, or because of personal reasons. [Client] must be aware of these reasons and the possibility that these could be challenged.

I enclose a copy of [client]'s draft will, which makes the following provisions:

1. [set out the terms of the draft will]

[client]'s present will makes the following provisions:

1. [set out the terms of the existing will]

Given the significance of the proposed changes to [client]'s will, [her] [his] medical diagnosis and the possibility of a claim being brought by [name], for example for insufficient financial provision or on the basis that [client] lacked capacity to amend [her] [his] will, the need for a detailed assessment of capacity is imperative.

Lasting Power of Attorney – Property & Financial Affairs

In relation to this particular decision, [client] will need to demonstrate that [s]he can answer the following questions:

1. What is a lasting power of attorney

2. Why does [s]he want to make a lasting power of attorney

3. Who is [s]he appointing as attorneys

4. Why [s]he has chosen those persons to act as [her] [his] attorneys

5. What is the nature and scope of the powers [s]he is giving to [her] [his] attorneys

Case law has also established that [client] will need to comprehend that [her] [his] attorneys will be able to assume complete authority over [her] [his] property and financial affairs and will be able to do anything with them which [s]he could have done, if [s]he is not capable of taking that particular decision [herself] [himself].

[Client] should also be able to appreciate that [her] [his] attorney's authority to make decisions will apply as soon as the lasting power of attorney is registered with the Office of the Public Guardian and will continue should [s]he lose mental capacity and that [s]he can only revoke [her] [his] lasting power of attorney while [s]he retains capacity to do so. [S]he should also understand the reasonably foreseeable consequences of making or not making the lasting power of attorney or making it on different terms or appointing different people.

Lasting Power of Attorney – Health & Welfare

The test in relation to the health and welfare lasting power of attorney is broadly as set out above, although of course it relates only to health and welfare matters. [Client] should appreciate that authority to make decisions will apply only if [s]he loses capacity to take decisions in respect of [her] [his] health and welfare and that the lasting power of attorney will enable [her] [his] attorneys to make decisions about anything that relates to [her] [his] health and welfare, for example medical matters, where [s]he should live and who [s]he should have contact with.

Gifts

The most important test on capacity to make a gift is *Re Beaney* (deceased). The judge in the case set out the following criteria for capacity to make a lifetime gift:

> "*The degree or extent of understanding required in respect of any instrument is relative to the particular transaction which it is to effect … Thus at one extreme, if the subject-matter and value of a gift are trivial in relation to the Donor's other assets, a low degree of understanding will suffice but, at the other, if its effect is to dispose of the Donor's only asset of value and thus, for practical purposes, to pre-empt the devolution of his estate under [the Donor's] Will or …*

intestacy, then the degree of understanding required is as high as that required for a Will, and the Donor must understand the claims of all potential Donees and the extent of the property to be disposed of".

To summarise, [client] should be aware of:

1. The nature of the transaction.
2. The effect of the transaction.
3. The extent of the property.
4. The claims to which [s]he ought to give effect.

By way of background to the proposed gift, [set out background].

I should be grateful if you would consider these three separate tests when you meet with [client]. It is possible that [s]he may have sufficient capacity to enter into some but not all of the transactions and you should therefore consider each decision separately.

Please do not hesitate to contact me should you have any queries.

Yours sincerely

APPENDIX 4

COURT OF PROTECTION APPLICATION FLOWCHART

Application

- COP1 in duplicate
- Relevant annex (e.g. COP1A, COP1E)
- COP3
- COP4 – deputyship applications
- COP12 – Trustee Act 1925 applications
- Application fee

↓

Application issued – service of P

- COP14 (serve personally on P) within 14 days of service of the application by the court
- COP20A return to the court within 7 days of service

↓

Application issued – service of others

- COP15 (serve in person, by first class post, fax or DX) within 14 days of service of the application by the court
- COP20B return to the court within 7 days of service

↓

Security bond (for deputyship applications only)

- Court will set the bond limit and advice as to how to obtain

APPENDIX 5

DEED OF APPOINTMENT OF NEW TRUSTEE PURSUANT TO SECTION 36(1) TRUSTEE ACT 1925

THIS DEED OF APPOINTMENT AND RETIREMENT is made the day of [year]

BETWEEN:—

(1) [NAME] of [address] ("**the Retiring Trustee**");

(2) [NAME] of [address] ("**the Continuing Trustee**")

(3) [NAME] of [address] ("**the New Trustee**");

WHEREAS:–

(1) This Deed is supplemental to a settlement dated [date] and made between [name] and [name] ("**the Settlement**").

(2) The Retiring Trustee is no longer capable of acting as trustee of the Settlement and the Continuing Trustee wishes to appoint the New Trustee to act as trustee of the Settlement jointly with the Continuing Trustee in place of the Retiring Trustee and the New Trustee has consented to act as trustee of the Settlement.

NOW THIS DEED WITNESSES as follows:—

1. In exercise of the power of appointment conferred upon him by section 36(1) Trustee Act 1925 and of every other power enabling him the Continuing Trustee hereby appoints the New Trustee to be trustee of the Settlement in place of the Retiring Trustee to act jointly with the Continuing Trustee.

2. The Retiring Trustee is hereby retired and is discharged from the trusts of the Settlement.

[3. The Continuing Trustee and the New Trustee jointly and severally covenant to indemnify and keep indemnified the Retiring Trustee and [his][her] estate from and against all liability arising in respect of the Settlement or arising out of the execution of this Deed, and all costs and expenses in connection with it.]

IN WITNESS the parties hereto have executed this Deed the day and year first above written

SIGNED AND DELIVERED by)

[NAME])

in the presence of:–) ……………………

Signature of Witness ……………………

Name ……………………

Address ……………………

……………………

Occupation ……………………

SIGNED AND DELIVERED by)

[NAME])

in the presence of:–) ……………………

Signature of Witness ……………………

Name ……………………

Address ....

....

Occupation ....

APPENDIX 6

PRECEDENT SECTION 54 TRUSTEE ACT 1925 ORDER

IN THE COURT OF PROTECTION

No.

MENTAL CAPACITY ACT 2005

IN THE MATTER OF

[NAME]

AND

[NAME]

ORDER UNDER SECTION 54 OF

THE TRUSTEE ACT 1925

Made by

At

On

WHEREAS

(1) An application has been made by [name] of [address] and [name] of [address] for new trustees to be appointed in relation to the trusts affecting [property address] registered under Title No [number] at HM Land Registry ("the trust property").

(2) The court is satisfied that there is reason to believe that [name] and [name] lack capacity in relation to the matter and considers it in their best interests to make this order without delay.

IT IS ORDERED THAT

1. **Appointment of new trustees**

(a) [name and address] [names and address] are appointed to be the new trustees in place of [name] and [name] in relation to the trusts affecting the trust property.

(b) The property subject to the trusts does now vest in the new trustees upon the subsisting trusts.

2. **Costs and expenses**

The costs of this application are fixed and to be paid equally from the assets of [name] and [name] but if the costs exceed the fixed amount they be agreed by the trustees and in default of agreement are to be subject to a detailed assessment on the standard basis. This order is to be treated as an authority to the Senior Court Costs Office to assess these costs.

3. **Right to apply for reconsideration of order**

This order was made without a hearing and without notice. Any person affected by this order may apply within 21 days of the date on which the order was served to have the order set aside or varied pursuant to Rule 14.3 of the Court of Protection Rules 2017 ("the Rules"). Such application must be made on Form COP9 and in accordance with Part 10 of the Rules.

APPENDIX 7

PRECEDENT SECTION 36(9) TRUSTEE ACT 1925 ORDER

IN THE COURT OF PROTECTION

No.

MENTAL CAPACITY ACT 2005

IN THE MATTER OF

[NAME]

ORDER UNDER SECTION 36(9) OF

THE TRUSTEE ACT 1925

Made by

At

On

WHEREAS

(1) An application has been made by [name] of [address] ("the Applicant") for a new trustee to be appointed in relation to the trusts affecting [property address] registered under Title No [number] at HM Land Registry ("the trust property").

(2) The court is satisfied that [name] is unable to make various decisions in relation to a matter or matters concerning property and affairs because of an impairment of, or a disturbance in the function of, the mind or brain and that the purpose for which the order is needed cannot be as effectively achieved in a way which is less restrictive of her rights and freedom of action.

IT IS ORDERED THAT

1. Appointment of new trustees

Permission is granted to [name of continuing trustee] of [address] in his capacity as continuing trustee to appoint [name] of [address] [and [name] of [address] as a new trustee in place of [name] in relation to the trusts affecting the trust property.

2. Costs and expenses

The costs of this application are fixed and to be paid from the assets of [name] but if the costs exceed the fixed amount they be agreed by the trustees and in default of agreement are to be subject to a detailed assessment on the standard basis. This order is to be treated as an authority to the Senior Court Costs Office to assess these costs.

3. Right to apply for reconsideration of order

This order was made without a hearing and without notice. Any person affected by this order may apply within 21 days of the date on which the order was served to have the order set aside or varied pursuant to Rule 14.3 of the Court of Protection Rules 2017 ("the Rules"). Such application must be made on Form COP9 and in accordance with Part 10 of the Rules.

APPENDIX 8

PRECEDENT DEPUTYSHIP ORDER

IN THE COURT OF PROTECTION

No.

MENTAL CAPACITY ACT 2005

IN THE MATTER OF

[NAME]

ORDER APPOINTING A DEPUTY FOR

PROPERTY AND AFFAIRS

Made by

At

On

UPON the Court being satisfied that [name] lacks capacity to make various decisions for [himself] [herself] in relation to a matter or matters concerning [his] [her] property and affairs, and that the purpose for which this order is needed cannot be effectively achieved in a way that is less restrictive of [his] [her] rights and freedom of action.

AND UPON the Court being satisfied that [name]'s interests and position can be properly secured without being joined to these proceedings and without making any further direction concerning [name]'s participation in these proceedings.

IT IS ORDERED THAT

1. **Appointment of [deputy] [joint deputies]**

(a) [N [s] and address[es] [is] [are] appointed [jointly] [jointly and severally] as [deputy] [deputies] [("the deputy")] [("the deputies")] to make decisions on behalf of [name] that [he] [she] is unable to make for [himself] [herself] in relation to [his] [her] property and affairs, subject to any conditions or restrictions set out in this order.

(b) The appointment will last until further Order.

(c) The [deputy] [deputies] must [jointly and severally] apply the principles set out in section 1 of the Mental Capacity Act 2005 ("the Act") and have regard to the guidance in the Code of Practice to the Act.

2. **Authority of [deputy] [deputies]**

(a) The court confers general authority on the [deputy] [deputies] to take possession or control of the property and affairs of [name] and to exercise the same powers of management and investment as [he] [she] has as beneficial owner, subject to the terms and conditions set out in this order.

(b) The [deputy] [deputies] cannot purchase any freehold or leasehold property on [name]'s behalf without obtaining further authority from the court.

(c) The [deputy] [deputies] must not sell, charge or otherwise dispose of any freehold or leasehold property in which [name[has a joint beneficial interest. An order authorising the appointment of a new trustee (or trustees) in place of [name] must be obtained before any sale or disposition of the property.

(d) If the [deputy] [deputies] consider it in [name]'s best interests to do so the deputy may appoint an investment manager, who is regulated and authorised to undertake investment business, to manage [his] [her] assets on a discretionary basis under the standard terms and conditions applicable to such service from to-to-time, and to permit the investments to be held in the name of the investment manager nominee company.

(e) The [deputy] [deputies] may make provision for the needs of anyone who is related to or connected with [name] if [he] [she] provided for, or might be expected to provide for, that person's needs by doing whatever [he] [she] did, or might reasonably be expected to do, to meet those needs.

(f) The [deputy] [deputies] may (without obtaining any further authority from the court) dispose of [name]'s money and property by way of gift to any charity to which [he] [she] made, or might have been expected to make, such gifts, and, on customary occasions, to persons who are related to or connected with [him] [her], provided that the value of each such gift is not unreasonable having regard to all the circumstances and, in particular, the size of [his] [her] estate.

(g) For the purpose of giving effect to any decision the [deputy] [deputies] may execute or sign any necessary deeds or documents.

3. Reports

(a) The [deputy is] [deputies are jointly] required to keep statements, vouchers, receipts and other financial records.

(b) The [deputy must] [deputies must jointly] submit an annual report to the Public Guardian as and when required to do so.

4. **Costs and expenses**

The [deputy is] [deputies are] authorised to pay [law firm] fixed costs for this application, or, where the amount exceeds the fixed costs allowed, the [deputy is] [deputies are] authorised to agree the costs for making this application and to pay them from funds belonging to [name]. In default of agreement, or if the deputy or the solicitors would prefer the costs to be assessed, this order is to be treated as authority to the Senior Court Costs Office to carry out a detailed assessment on the standard basis.

6. **Security**

(a) The [deputy is] [deputies are jointly] required forthwith to obtain and maintain security in the sum of £[sum] in accordance with the standard requirements as to the giving of security.

(b) The [deputy] [deputies] must ensure that the level of security ordered by the court is in place before discharging any of the functions conferred by this order.

7. **Notification**

The [deputy] [deputies] must, within 14 days of service of this order by the court, notify [name] personally that the court has made a decision by providing [him] [her] with a notice of proceedings about you in the Court of Protection (form COP14) and a copy of this Order. The requirement for the person effecting notification of the issue of this order to provide the court with a certificate of notification is dispensed with.

8. **Right to apply for reconsideration of order**

This order was made without a hearing and without notice. Any person affected by this order may apply within 21 days of the date on which this order was served to have the order set aside or varied pursuant to Rule 13.4 of the Court of Protection Rules 2017 ("the Rules"). Such application must be made on Form COP9 and in accordance with Part 10 of the Rules.

APPENDIX 9

ORDERS SOUGHT FROM THE COURT OF PROTECTION (BOX 4.1 COP1)

Authority of deputy/ies

- A declaration that P lacks mental capacity to manage his or her affairs

- To confer general authority on the [deputy] [deputies] to take possession or control of the property and affairs of [name] and to exercise the same powers of management and investment, as [he] [she] has as beneficial owner

- The [deputy] [deputies] may make provision for the needs of anyone who is related to or connected with [name] if [he] [she] provided for, or might be expected to provide for, that person's needs by doing whatever [he] [she] did, or might reasonably be expected to do, to meet those needs

- The [deputy] [deputies] may (without obtaining any further authority from the court) dispose of [name]'s money and property by way of gift to any charity to which [he] [she] made, or might have been expected to make, such gifts, and, on customary occasions, to persons who are related to or connected with [him] [her], provided that the value of each such gift is not unreasonable having regard to all the circumstances and, in particular, the size of [his] [her] estate

- For the purpose of giving effect to any decision the [deputy] [deputies] may execute or sign any necessary deeds or documents

- To authorise the [deputy] [deputies] to sell the property of [name] known as [address of property] on the best possible terms and after payment of legal fees and other professional charges to invest the net proceeds for [name]'s benefit

- To authorise the [deputy] [deputies] to purchase and freehold or leasehold property on [name]'s behalf without obtaining further authority of the court

- Authority for the [deputy] [deputies] to take such steps as may be necessary to obtain (either alone or with a co-administrator) a grant of representation to the estate of [name] and to use the share to which [name] is entitled for [his] [her] benefit

- The [deputy is] [deputies are] authorised to pay [law firm] fixed costs for this application, or, where the amount exceeds the fixed costs allowed, the [deputy is] [deputies are] authorised to agree the costs for making this application and to pay them from funds belonging to [name]. In default of agreement, or if the deputy or the solicitors would prefer the costs to be assessed, this order is to be treated as authority to the Senior Court Costs Office to carry out a detailed assessment on the standard basis.

- The [deputy is] [deputies are] authorised, with retrospective effect as necessary, to instruct [name] to advise and assist in respect of issuing arising in connection with [detail]. In order to give effect to this authority, the [deputy is] [deputies are] authorised to use funds of [name] up to a limit of £[amount]. (For the avoidance of doubt, this authority does not extend to the issue or conduct of proceedings in respect of [name].)

- In so far as the authority granted by paragraph [number] above is retrospective, the costs already incurred by the [deputy] [deputies] shall be subject to detailed assessment by the Senior Courts Costs Office on the standard basis. The [deputy is] [deputies are] authorised to make from the funds of [name] a payment on account not exceeding 75% + VAT of the total sum authorised in paragraph [number] above, pending assessment.

- The [deputy is] [deputies are] authorised to obtain Counsel's opinion (including by conference, and including paying the costs of attendance at such conference by [name]) on matters relating to [name]. In order to give effect to this authority the [deputy is] [deputies are] authorised to use funds of [name] up to a total limit of £[amount].

- To authorise the [deputy] [deputies] to conduct proceedings in the name of and on behalf of [name] and to act therein in litigation friend in relation to [detail]

- To authorise the [deputy] [deputies] to act as litigation friend for [name] in the divorce and financial remedies proceedings and to approval any financial settlement

- To authorise the [deputy] [deputies] to conduct proceeds as litigation friend in the name of and on behalf of [name] under the Inheritance {Provision for Family and Dependents) Act 1975

- The [deputy] [deputies] be authorised to realise £[amount] by entering into an equity release scheme over the property known as [address] and prepare a trust deed to protect [name]'s beneficial interest in the property

- The [deputy] [deputies] be authorised in the name of and on behalf of [name] [jointly with] to enter into a mortgage of the [jointly owned] property with [lender] and to execute any necessary documents.

MORE BOOKS BY LAW BRIEF PUBLISHING

A selection of our other titles available now:-

‘Covid-19, Homeworking and the Law – The Essential Guide to Employment and GDPR Issues’ by Forbes Solicitors
‘Covid-19, Force Majeure and Frustration of Contracts – The Essential Guide’ by Keith Markham
‘Covid-19 and Criminal Law – The Essential Guide’ by Ramya Nagesh
‘Covid-19 and Family Law in England and Wales – The Essential Guide’ by Safda Mahmood
‘A Practical Guide to the Law of Unlawful Eviction and Harassment – 2nd Edition’ by Stephanie Lovegrove
‘Covid-19, Residential Property, Equity Release and Enfranchisement – The Essential Guide’ by Paul Sams and Louise Uphill
‘Covid-19, Brexit and the Law of Commercial Leases – The Essential Guide’ by Mark Shelton
‘A Practical Guide to Costs in Personal Injury Claims – 2nd Edition’ by Matthew Hoe
‘A Practical Guide to the General Data Protection Regulation (GDPR) – 2nd Edition’ by Keith Markham
‘Ellis on Credit Hire – Sixth Edition’ by Aidan Ellis & Tim Kevan
‘A Practical Guide to Working with Litigants in Person and McKenzie Friends in Family Cases’ by Stuart Barlow
‘Protecting Unregistered Brands: A Practical Guide to the Law of Passing Off’ by Lorna Brazell
‘A Practical Guide to Secondary Liability and Joint Enterprise Post-Jogee’ by Joanne Cecil & James Mehigan
‘A Practical Guide to the Pre-Action RTA Claims Protocol for Personal Injury Lawyers’ by Antonia Ford
‘A Practical Guide to Neighbour Disputes and the Law’ by Alexander Walsh
‘A Practical Guide to Forfeiture of Leases’ by Mark Shelton
‘A Practical Guide to Coercive Control for Legal Practitioners and Victims’ by Rachel Horman

'A Practical Guide to Rights Over Airspace and Subsoil' by Daniel Gatty
'Tackling Disclosure in the Criminal Courts – A Practitioner's Guide' by Narita Bahra QC & Don Ramble
'A Practical Guide to the Law of Driverless Cars – Second Edition' by Alex Glassbrook, Emma Northey & Scarlett Milligan
'A Practical Guide to TOLATA Claims' by Greg Williams
'Artificial Intelligence – The Practical Legal Issues' by John Buyers
'A Practical Guide to the Law of Prescription in Scotland' by Andrew Foyle
'A Practical Guide to the Construction and Rectification of Wills and Trust Instruments' by Edward Hewitt
'A Practical Guide to the Law of Bullying and Harassment in the Workplace' by Philip Hyland
'How to Be a Freelance Solicitor: A Practical Guide to the SRA-Regulated Freelance Solicitor Model' by Paul Bennett
'A Practical Guide to Prison Injury Claims' by Malcolm Johnson
'A Practical Guide to the Small Claims Track' by Dominic Bright
'A Practical Guide to Advising Clients at the Police Station' by Colin Stephen McKeown-Beaumont
'A Practical Guide to Antisocial Behaviour Injunctions' by Iain Wightwick
'Practical Mediation: A Guide for Mediators, Advocates, Advisers, Lawyers, and Students in Civil, Commercial, Business, Property, Workplace, and Employment Cases' by Jonathan Dingle with John Sephton
'The Mini-Pupillage Workbook' by David Boyle
'A Practical Guide to Crofting Law' by Brian Inkster
'A Practical Guide to Spousal Maintenance' by Liz Cowell
'A Practical Guide to the Law of Domain Names and Cybersquatting' by Andrew Clemson
'A Practical Guide to the Law of Gender Pay Gap Reporting' by Harini Iyengar

'A Practical Guide to the Rights of Grandparents in Children Proceedings' by Stuart Barlow
'NHS Whistleblowing and the Law' by Joseph England
'Employment Law and the Gig Economy' by Nigel Mackay & Annie Powell
'A Practical Guide to Noise Induced Hearing Loss (NIHL) Claims' by Andrew Mckie, Ian Skeate, Gareth McAloon
'An Introduction to Beauty Negligence Claims – A Practical Guide for the Personal Injury Practitioner' by Greg Almond
'Intercompany Agreements for Transfer Pricing Compliance' by Paul Sutton
'Zen and the Art of Mediation' by Martin Plowman
'A Practical Guide to the SRA Principles, Individual and Law Firm Codes of Conduct 2019 – What Every Law Firm Needs to Know' by Paul Bennett
'A Practical Guide to Adoption for Family Lawyers' by Graham Pegg
'A Practical Guide to Industrial Disease Claims' by Andrew Mckie & Ian Skeate
'A Practical Guide to Redundancy' by Philip Hyland
'A Practical Guide to Vicarious Liability' by Mariel Irvine
'A Practical Guide to Applications for Landlord's Consent and Variation of Leases' by Mark Shelton
'A Practical Guide to Relief from Sanctions Post-Mitchell and Denton' by Peter Causton
'A Practical Guide to Equity Release for Advisors' by Paul Sams
'A Practical Guide to the Law Relating to Food' by Ian Thomas
'A Practical Guide to Financial Services Claims' by Chris Hegarty
'The Law of Houses in Multiple Occupation: A Practical Guide to HMO Proceedings' by Julian Hunt
'A Practical Guide to Unlawful Eviction and Harassment' by Stephanie Lovegrove
'Occupiers, Highways and Defective Premises Claims: A Practical Guide Post-Jackson – 2nd Edition' by Andrew Mckie

www.ingramcontent.com/pod-product-compliance
Lightning Source LLC
LaVergne TN
LVHW050303210926
848481LV00014BA/814
* 9 7 8 1 9 1 3 7 1 5 7 5 5 *